WITH THIS RING

WITH THIS RING

Marian Wells

BETHANY HOUSE PUBLISHERS
MINNEAPOLIS, MINNESOTA 55438

MARIAN WELLS and her husband live in Boulder, Colorado, which gives her immediate access to the research and documentation of the historical surroundings of this book and the books to follow in this series. A well-known author, her research and background on Mormonism provided the thrust for her bestselling STARLIGHT TRILOGY, the *Wedding Dress* and *With This Ring*.

Manuscript edited by Penelope J. Stokes.

Cover illustration by Dan Thornberg,
Bethany House Publishers staff artist.

Published by Bethany House Publishers
A Division of Bethany Fellowship, Inc.
6820 Auto Club Road, Minneapolis, MN 55438

Printed in the United States of America

Library of Congress Cataloging in Publication Data

Wells, Marian, 1931–
   With this ring.

   I. Title.
PS3573.E4927W5   1984   813'.54   84–9301
ISBN 0–87123–615–X

PREFACE

The preceding story, *The Wedding Dress*, centers around Rebecca Wolstone's early years. In 1831, the same year the Church of Jesus Christ of Latter-Day Saints was organized, she was born in New York. Rebecca's earliest memories were of life on the mud flats of the Mississippi River, near a community that was soon to become the Mormon city of Nauvoo, Illinois.

Those mud flats robbed Rebecca of her family. The Wolstones, along with many of their neighbors, fell victim to the swift and deadly cholera. Like many of the other children left orphaned that year, Rebecca was taken into one of the neighboring homes in the community. The Smyths were kind to the young girl, but she never forgot that she was one more mouth to feed in a poor, hungry family of young ones. Neither quite a family member nor a comfortable guest, Rebecca grew up without really having a sense of belonging.

In 1844, the year of Rebecca's thirteenth birthday, two events profoundly touched and changed her life. That spring 17-year-old Joshua Smyth, the eldest son in the family and Rebecca's dearest friend, left Illinois to find a niche for himself (and, eventually, the rest of his family) in Oregon Territory. When he left, his eyes promised Rebecca what his words dared not say, and Rebecca was filled with both desolation and hope.

Meanwhile, the Mormon Church had from the beginning faced persecution and rejection. In Nauvoo, no less than any other place, the Saints were living an uneasy existence.

When Joseph Smith, founder and president of the church, and his brother Hyrum were murdered just miles from Nauvoo, Rebecca Wolstone's attention and sympathies were captured. And when the Saints left Illinois for the Great Basin in the far West, Rebecca was numbered among them.

Great Salt Lake City became Rebecca's new home. Under the watchful eye of Brigham Young, subject to the doctrines of the Mormon Church, Rebecca struggled to be a good schoolteacher and to learn to conform to the church. But her "rebellious" ways merited her the discipline of a move south to the frontier town of Cedar City.

For Rebecca had balked at becoming a plural wife. In this "doctrine," the church declared, God had revealed His highest plan for His people: only through "celestial marriage" could a man achieve the highest heaven. This doctrine, including plural marriage and blood atonement, is still found in the DOCTRINE AND COVENANTS.

The Principle, as the doctrine of plural marriage was called, had been practiced covertly from the earliest days of the church. Only after the Saints had moved to the Great Basin did the church leaders feel secure enough to reveal to the world that doctrine which they had been denying publicly from the very beginning. To the federal government, plural marriage was illegal, and any children of such unions had no legal rights in the nation or as heirs. No wonder, then, that few women had accepted Brigham Young's generous offer of "freedom," extended that October conference of 1856. Outside the Territory they would have been considered prostitutes with illegitimate children.

Brigham Young's unhappy wife number 27, Ann Eliza, divorced him and tried to sue for an enormous settlement. While recognizing that the United States courts gave no legal recognition to polygamy, he made a magnanimous offer of $200,000 in settlement of the suit, with the provision that the courts must legitimatize all Mormon plural marriages by declaring his marriage to Ann Eliza legal. The court was unwilling and unable to do so.

The accepted practice among the Saints was to include the first wife as a participant in subsequent marriage ceremonies. But occasionally, as in Rebecca's case, the marriages were made without informing the women of the existence of other wives.

Rebecca, caught in such a marriage, eventually rebelled despite her original resolve to conform and accept the teaching of the church. In the midst of her struggle, Rebecca began to search for God, a search which led her away from Mormon teachings and nearly cost her life.

In an Indian camp, Joshua Smyth found Rebecca recovering from a near-fatal gunshot wound inflicted by her Mormon husband, and planned to take her with him back to Oregon. Throughout the years, he had demonstrated his faithful friendship as well as a deep sense of responsibility for Rebecca's welfare.

With This Ring takes up the story of Rebecca's new life. As she leaves the desert country of Southern Utah, she begins the move from barrenness to hope. But will she ever be truly beyond the reach of her former church?

Books by Marian Wells

The Wedding Dress
With This Ring

Karen

The STARLIGHT TRILOGY Series
    The Wishing Star
    Star Light, Star Bright
    Morning Star

The TREASURE QUEST Series
    Colorado Gold
    Out of the Crucible
    The Silver Highway
    Jewel of Promise

CHAPTER 1

Rebecca could smell the pungent smoke of the pine and sage fire. Bitter cold won out over its feeble warmth, and she buried her nose in the rabbit-skin robe. Snuggling deeper into the robe, she felt sleep claiming her again.

The resinous pine snapped like gunfire and, with a cry of terror, she struggled against the blackness of the dream trying to suck her downward. Even as she fought against its fearful scenes, part of her mind reminded her that it was only a dream, the same one repeated endlessly throughout the days of her illness. But even now that she had strength to contend with the terror of memory, there was still only one escape.

Fighting off the heavy robes and blankets, Rebecca threw herself from her bed mat. Solali, crouched beside the fire, turned with a concerned frown to watch Rebecca. Shivering now, Rebecca pushed aside the heavy mass of blonde hair from her face and knelt beside the Indian woman. She wiped the perspiration from her face while Solali's troubled eyes studied her. " 'Tis the dream?"

Rebecca nodded tremulously and held her hands toward the blaze. "That cracklin' log did it. Seemed like rifle fire, and—and I was back there, livin' it over." She was trembling now and Solali reached for the blanket.

More cold air struck Rebecca at the same time she heard Joshua whispering from the doorway. "Solali, I've got to talk to Rebecca." As she turned, the deerskin curtain covering the doorway of the hut was pulled aside as Joshua stepped through

9

the opening and saw her. "You're up early this cold morning. Did you feel the touch of snow in the air?"

Still caught in the terror of the dream, she whispered dully, "Snow?"

It was Solali who saw his worried eyes fixed on Rebecca and moved closer. "Eagle?" she asked. He hesitated for a moment and then turned to the Indian woman.

"Solali, we've got to get out of here," he murmured. "There's trouble a'brewing but plenty."

"Where's Eagle?" she asked again.

"He's here, just come back. That's why—"

Rebecca moved slowly. Turning from the fire, still shivering, she clutched the blanket about her, but she lifted her chin and said, "It's bad, and I might as well know about it. You two have been whispering behind my back for long enough. 'Tis time I start livin' again." Her voice caught; she took two quick nervous steps toward the door and then returned to the fire.

She faced Joshua and, for the first time, saw the lines of fatigue on his face. As she studied those lines, wondering at their meaning, Eagle came into the hut. Moving to the other side of the fire, he squatted and held his hands toward the warmth.

Joshua knelt beside him, and while the two men spoke in low, hurried tones, Rebecca watched Eagle. She was still frowning at what she saw when Joshua got to his feet and came back to her. "Eagle's tired," she said, "and I know he's been gone someplace." She faced Joshua. "You look like something's pressing upon you."

The curtain swung softly into place again as Eagle left the hut. Joshua's worried frown was still on his face as he turned, and pulling off his hat, tossed it to the stack of robes. Though dressed like a native American, his golden hair and beard caught the light and sharpened the contrast between the Indians and himself. Rebecca thought of the strange picture she, too, created. Her heavy blonde hair was braided Indian-style and she was wearing the typical Paiute woman's dress. A tentative smile curved her lips.

Joshua bent down beside her and looked into her face. His

smile reflected not so much amusement or joy but simply relief at her softened expression. Knowing why, Rebecca stretched out her hand in mute apology. Joshua squeezed her hand but said abruptly, "Becky, I want you to get your things together right now. We're leaving as soon as we can get packs on the horses."

"Leaving!" Jumping to her feet and spinning away from the fire, she looked wildly about the smoke-filled hut. From the soft couch of rabbit-skin robes which had been her sanctuary since Eagle had carried her unconscious and wounded to the Indian village, to the mounds of pelts for barter and the storage baskets holding their winter provisions of food, this humble hut had been home. She reached out to stroke the curved walls, saplings woven into protection against the elements.

"Leave," she whispered again, her voice reflecting disbelief. She trembled to think of that world beyond the confines of the village. "No!" Her voice out of control, she pressed her knuckles against her lips and tried to calm herself.

"Becky, Rebecca," Joshua pleaded, his voice both placating and firm. "There's to be no arguing. I didn't ask. I'm tellin'. I'd be obliged if you'd ask no questions. There isn't time. Just get your things together." He turned to Solali, "Please—"

"I go too." Shaking her head, Rebecca tried to grasp the Indian woman's arm. Ignoring Rebecca, Solali continued, "You need help."

"I do, more than—" He swallowed hard. Abruptly he got to his feet and reached for his hat. As he left the hut Solali followed him out into the crisp morning air.

Flakes of snow were beginning to obscure the sky. Joshua watched them swirl about and turned to Solali. " 'Tis terrible weather for anybody to be startin' a journey. I'm wondering if Rebecca will make it. If you'll be telling me no, well, I'll be settin' my mind to some other solution."

For a moment Solali stared up at him. Her reply was simple. "Indians don't stay in the mountains during the cold times. Soon the Saints will be wondering why the village has not moved down to the warm, dry desert. Then they will visit the village, and they will find your Becky."

For a long moment Joshua was silent; then slowly and deliberately he spoke. "She's thin and frail. That whiteness and the terrible stillness inside scares me, but I'd rather have her die in my arms halfway to Oregon than to have them get their hands on her."

"Then we go."

They both heard the gasp and turned. Rebecca was standing in the doorway, clutching the deerskin curtain with both hands.

Joshua moved toward her. "Becky, you'll need to hear me out. Go back inside; you'll freeze out here." He pushed at her motionless form and beckoned to Solali.

Inside, on the bed of coals, the pot of water was boiling. Solali moved past Rebecca and Joshua. They watched her kneel beside the fire and stir meal into the pot.

Now Rebecca was aware of Joshua's scrutiny; reluctantly she turned to face him. Speaking slowly as he studied her face, he said, "Eagle's come with news. You've got to understand, Becky, this isn't my own idea. I'd be willin' to stay here 'til warm weather, but 'tisn't safe."

He paused to pace the tiny circle around the fire before adding, "The dear Lord knows I'm worried about the trip and a'wishin' there would be a spot in the Territory where you'd be safe." He deliberately stopped in front of her and stared intently down at her. "You understand what I'm saying, don't you?"

With a sigh she turned away. A touch of bitterness colored her voice as she replied, "I'm knowin' well."

For a moment he measured her fear and bitterness against what he must say. Trying to soften the impact, he touched her shoulder. "Now you'll hear me out. Eagle's been riding the Territory these past weeks, doing the scouting I dare not do." She looked up with a surprised frown and he explained, "You need to know, Brigham Young has cracked down on every stranger in the Territory. He's issuin' permits to all the travelers hereabouts. I'm understanding, from all that's been told me, that it bodes no good for the man without one. That's another reason we must leave, and quickly. Every day we wait, we stand a greater chance of being challenged by one of his men when we *do* try to go."

Restlessly he paced to the door. "I wish Eagle would come back. I sent him to round up some horses." When he returned to the fire, he saw Rebecca's face lifted to him, the face of a bewildered, lost child.

"Another reason?" she whispered. "Then there's more bad news you've had."

Nodding curtly he faced her and said, "You know since last summer President Buchanan has had federal troops moving this way. They say it's nothing to be feared, it's only the normal thing, and I believed it so. Oregon Territory was right proud to have the troops and the colors on its home ground. Makes a body feel protected. Seems here it was taken all wrong."

Rebecca agreed, her tone dark, " 'Tis *all* taken wrong. Everything the government has done rubs them the wrong way. Brigham's fought it all, saying he'll be governor regardless. Why don't they just leave the man alone for the sake of peace?"

Joshua hesitated and peered at Rebecca. When he answered her his voice was flat, low, "Seems you've been whipped beyond reason."

"I've not," she replied, astonished.

"You're not understandin'. I'm thinkin' you've been beaten down more than you know." After a moment he continued, "Hear me out. Brigham's Nauvoo Legion has been standing off the troops. It's bad enough that he's plugged up Echo Canyon with them, but now Eagle says Young's had them harassing the army all winter. First the Mormons burned the supply trains. When Johnston tried to enter Utah by way of the Soda Springs road, they ran off cattle and blocked his way. Then the weather settled in. While he was hightailing back to Fort Bridger, he lost a goodly share of his stock. Now I'm hearin' that five hundred head of oxen and fifty-seven head of mules and horses froze to death on the Sweetwater. Another five hundred head froze before they made it back to their winter quarters."

He hesitated, then said dryly, "I'm not thinkin' all that stock came along just for the trip. Seems the resistance is a pretty drastic step to take against the whole United States government. There's bound to be problems. I hear the Mormons have burned out Fort Bridger long ago, so that's meanin' the troops spent a miserable winter up there. Now Eagle's sayin' there's new rumbles. In Great Salt Lake City they were getting all ready to start celebrating the spring victory in advance when they heard there's troops a'movin' up the Colorado River."

"Joshua," Rebecca gasped, "that's nearly in our backyard!"

He nodded. "And it's more'n a rumor. I don't know who they are, and I'm not so sure they're troops, but Eagle has spotted them. He followed a scouting party up the Colorado. Says they're gettin' mighty close to the Virgin River."

"Do the Saints know?"

"Yes. Eagle said Hamblin's men were moseyin' right along behind them."

Joshua watched Rebecca as she stared into the flickering fire. Slowly her hand crept to her throat. "What are you thinkin'?" he asked quietly.

"I'm feeling so sorry for all those people—my neighbors and friends." She shook her head wearily. "The good people, the followers. It's just like before. Like Ohio and Missouri and Illinois. I'm guessing how badly they're feeling this—the upset and the fear. Now they'll be pressed to the wall again." She sighed and shook her head, "That proud angry man! Last summer Brigham had them ready to set fire to their homes and destroy everything they've slaved to accomplish—all rather than to settle back and obey the laws of the country. They'll run always. For the rest of their lives they'll run if someone doesn't talk sense into that man."

"I'm not understandin' why the people stand for it," Joshua said slowly, his voice rough with worry. "These are free people. Why don't they rise up for their own good and fight for their rights?"

"Free?" Rebecca's voice was scornful. "They aren't free. They've been taught to obey or they'll be damned." She waved her hand. "See, just like Heber Kimball said, Brigham Young is god to them. And Joseph Smith was god to the people while he was alive."

"Rebecca," Joshua was speaking carefully. "Do you understand? They're coming this way." He hesitated, watching Rebecca as she began to comprehend it all.

"You're meaning them all. The people in Great Salt Lake City and Brigham Young and the twelve. All of them."

He added, "With troops moving up the rivers and pressing in from the east, this Territory will be overrun."

She was whispering as if even now they could hear her. "Where will they go? The only place left is to run to the desert. Those people, all the people, from all those towns—Provo, even Cedar, Parowan, Pinto, Harmony." She pressed trembling hands against her cheeks. Her eyes were darkening as she fought to take deep, calm breaths. As he saw how pale her face was becoming, he found himself doubly determined to leave immediately.

At his shoulder Solali whispered, "Bad as the dreams, it is." He looked at her dark, brooding face and she said, "I go, too."

He stepped closer to Rebecca. "It's only February, there's snow and cold. It'll be fearsome until we reach the Willamette. The dear Lord knows I intended to wait until spring—now we dare not. Becky, we must leave *now*."

She roused herself and shook her head. She was looking as if she had just awakened, her eyes widening.

"Joshua, I'll never make it. You go, you'll be running for your life. I mustn't hold you back."

"Rebecca," he bent over her. "I didn't come this far just to give up now. No matter how weak you are, you must go. I'll get you through. One thing I know, every hour we delay cuts our chances of making it safely."

With that face so close, those eyes demanding, Rebecca merely nodded as she dabbed at the weak tears on her cheeks. He remained close and in the chill of the hut, she was aware of his warmth, feeling the strength of him pressing through her coldness and fear to give her hope.

Solali repeated, "I go, too." Rebecca lifted her head and shook it but Solali insisted. "I fear, too. Remember last year and the reformation, the blood atonement. There's danger still." Her dark eyes were flashing as she whispered, "Not any of us rebellious ones will be safe. What happened can happen again."

Rebecca faced Solali and thoughtfully studied the woman. Without a doubt Solali, another former plural wife, was in as much danger as she was. They were both rebellious ones. "Yes," Rebecca put into words her thoughts and again the bitterness came through. "An Indian, raised and educated by the Saints. Privileged to be a plural wife, and now you're choosing to deny it all—at the risk of your life."

Rebecca's eyes widened with growing fear for the woman as she thought about Solali's history.

Orphaned in early youth, the Indian girl had been sold to the Mormons as a slave. But the Saints, in accordance with their beliefs, had raised her as a member of the family until she was old enough to become a plural wife.

Now Rebecca must ask the question that had been on her mind for some time. "Do you miss it, Solali?" she whispered. "Do you miss the other life?"

Slowly Solali turned, and with a puzzled frown she studied Rebecca's face before saying, "The snug cabins and the milk and yeasty bread, I do. I liked caring for the gardens and chickens and cows. But I didn't like the other."

"Say it," Rebecca demanded.

"I didn't like being one of many wives. I didn't like—" She gestured wordlessly and Rebecca finished for her.

"You've said it before. Sharing a man, being scorned because there was no child. You said it was like having a string tied around you, being jerked at will, knowing only that life was a set of rules."

Now Solali added, "They told me I must not forget my past. I must be good so that I would turn white and pure. I must follow the prophet or be damned.'"

"And you want to live like this again?" Rebecca gestured toward the simple shelter.

She nodded, "And I'm remembering you left, too," Solali whispered. Rebecca felt herself writhing away from the memories, but the Indian woman persisted. "You won't go back. You had Eagle bring the trunk. You touch the Book with faraway eyes. But I see much fear. Is that a good thing in exchange? If it were only fear keeping me here, I could not stay."

While they had been talking Eagle slipped back into the hut. Rebecca glanced at him, wondering how much he understood. This silent Indian with the serene eyes seemed to always be there. Twice within the past year he had saved her life. Yet in the depths of his stoic face there was nothing to reveal his thoughts or feelings. As she studied him, briefly their eyes met and he turned away. She bit her lip, wanting desperately to say to him what she was feeling so deeply, the gratitude.

Looking around the hut, thinking of the people who had touched her life in this place, Rebecca was conscious of a wrenching, a feeling of saying good-bye to all that had been her life for the past months. It was the leaving-home feeling. Wordlessly she stretched her hand toward Eagle, wondering how she would ever repay his kindness.

Joshua got to his feet. He sighed, then with an attempt at lightness, said, "Tuck that Bible back in the trunk with the wedding dress and be ready to leave when the sun clears the trees."

CHAPTER 2

Joshua, aware that Solali had followed him out of the hut, waited until Eagle strode out of sight before turning to her.

She was shaking her head. "Joshua, it's a fearsome thing you're asking of her."

"She's far from well." He shook his head in frustration.

"More than that," Solali insisted anxiously, "there are deep shadows in her spirit. She thinks I don't see, but I've watched her with the Book. Such sadness. Almost—almost, I think she doesn't believe the words now."

A shaft of pale sunlight pierced the trees and Joshua moved impatiently. "Solali, we must go. I'm obliged to you for coming with us." She was nodding as she started back to the hut. He added, "Eagle is going to travel with us too." Her outstretched hand clutched the deerskin curtain. He noticed and asked, "That troubles you?"

Without facing him, she replied, "No. But I do wish to see him forget me." She disappeared behind the curtain. Joshua stood for a moment longer, pondering her reaction to the handsome young Indian.

In the few short months since he had come to the Indian village, Joshua had learned to trust and respect the young man with the deep, expressive eyes. His quiet presence managed to communicate to Joshua a loyal friendship that he was coming to depend upon with increasing gratitude. Although the words between them were few because of Eagle's limited English, both of them were beginning to sense the spirit of the other. As time went on, Joshua was realizing how really unnecessary words were.

Solali paused just inside the hut and looked at Rebecca standing beside the fire with tears rolling down her cheeks. She was pressing her hands against her thin waist.

"You are in pain?" Solali whispered as she watched Rebecca move the fingers of her left hand slowly down her right side. Even as Rebecca shook her head, Solali said, "The wound was bad; that angry red scar will be with you forever."

Rebecca rubbed her hands across her tear-streaked cheeks and in a voice thick with grief said, "I was just remembering. Seems I must remind myself every day. When I don't, I catch myself reaching to feel my baby, and finding only the emptiness and the scar." Now she turned quickly as if to throw off the darkness that gripped her. "Solali, I'm not once forgetting the way you've taken care of me. I guess those bad times will always be with me, but I try, I really do, to think of you instead and the way you were always there when I cried or when the dream came." Rebecca reached toward the Indian woman.

Solali hesitated and then in a low voice said, "You remind me that I am Indian, that I don't hug and kiss like the Saints." She reached out and patted Rebecca's face and while Rebecca clung to her hand, she promised, "I'll still be there when you need me. I don't know why it must be, but I cannot let you go alone."

It was past midday when the six horses left the mountain trail and headed north. Joshua knew that soon the road they followed would wind past the trail cutting down into Mountain Meadows. Would Becky recognize it?

The memory of all that he had heard about the massacre struck him, and he caught his breath as the images filled his thoughts and set him trembling with anger.

Wheeling his horse back to Rebecca's mount, he leaned forward, but she turned her anguished face away from him. He hunched down in the saddle, helplessly at loss for the right words. "This is the first time you've been back here since . . . isn't it?" he asked in a troubled voice, thinking of Eagle carrying her to the Indian village, wounded and about to deliver her child.

As he continued to study her, Joshua realized he had been so concerned about her weak body that he hadn't considered the emotional impact of the familiar miles upon her.

Solali pulled her horse even with them and with a relieved sigh, Joshua dropped back. When Rebecca briefly raised her head, he saw the shine of moisture on her cheeks.

He caught Eagle's quick glance, and although Joshua knew the man probably didn't understand him, he said, "Somehow I'm not much good at these women problems."

They were well on the other side of the trail, moving west, when Rebecca broke the long silence. "I'm thinking I must look very strange dressed in this manner."

"You're wanting to wear that calico dress?" Joshua tried for a light touch as he referred to the garment he had previously purchased for Rebecca from an Indian in the village.

"You look like a young Indian boy from a distance," Solali said and added, "We must keep you that way."

There was a thoughtful expression in Rebecca's eyes. She said, "Then it's no accident you've chosen this dark hunk of fur to cover my hair. It's no accident it hangs nearly to my nose. I was guessing it was to keep me warm. Now I understand." The chill in her voice made Joshua almost frantic with despair.

"Becky"—Joshua's tone was impatient, ragged—"it's only in case. You're safe now. Besides, most travelers have enough gumption to stay at home in weather like this." He squinted at the leaden sky as a few more flakes of snow landed in his beard.

"It's a lonesome road we're setting out on," she whispered. "All because of me, my friends must suffer."

"And me," Solali added. "You forget, I've as much reason to leave as you."

"And me," Joshua said, forcing a twisted grin. "With Brigham's crackdown on every stranger in the Territory, and with whispers coming up the Colorado, we're smart to hightail out of the Territory as fast as we can go."

"All except Eagle." Rebecca turned to study the impassive face of the bronzed man who had first come into her life long ago when he rescued her and her milk cow from the mountains near Pinto. "Only Eagle has no reason to run with the rest."

The Indian glanced at her, and a tiny smile tugged at his gentle face. She found herself wondering again how much of the conversation he really understood.

"I think we'd better hurry along." Joshua's words interrupted her thoughts. "This snow is going to be a good storm yet. Even with the best of luck, we'll be spending the night under the sagebrush."

Rebecca shivered and pulled the rabbit-skin robe over the buckskin pants and shirt she wore. "Well, no matter, dressing like a little Indian boy is warmer than struggling with the calico, no matter how pretty it is."

"We'll be hard pressed to explain you once we hit civilization."

"There's people living out this way?" Rebecca asked slowly.

He nodded. Watching the play of expression on her face, he realized she had not thought about the journey that lay ahead of them. "We'll be traveling in Utah Territory for a piece. I've gone the route many a time, taking this trail up toward the Oregon cutoff. I've traveled the Salt Lake-California cutoff too."

"If there's settlements out this way, and this is Utah Territory, then —"

"You're wrong," he cut through her words, guessing the direction her thoughts were carrying her. "This isn't farming land we'll be crossing. It's desert. Except for trading posts and way stations for the freighters, there's scarcely a cabin. You're thinking of Mormon Station. That's snugged up against the Sierras, and we'll go nowhere close to it."

"It's a lonesome land." She glanced quickly at their two companions, remembering the Indian stories she had heard. Would Eagle's and Solali's presence assure their safe passage?

"That's not so. The land's been crisscrossed with trails since the late twenties. You can't feel too lonesome when you find a trail and then see a discarded barrel or even a piece of furniture, though that's not likely. Most of the discards end up being used for firewood."

"What about water?"

"In the summer you best stick to the main routes and hope your animals last between water holes and grass. Winter isn't too bad if you find forage. Winter, there's water holes that never exist in the summer. It's the clay in the soil. It collects and holds the water from runoff."

The snow ended and the sky cleared. They rode across land sparsely covered with sage and salt grass. Occasional sandy hills nurtured struggling plant life in their sheltering clasp, but across the open desert, crimped by distant jagged peaks, they moved in the full blast of the sandy wind.

Their diagonal journey, marked on a northwestern slant toward Oregon, seemed to be a dream of unyielding dimensions. The clumps of sage and infrequent juniper stands were approached and left behind, but the distant mountains seemed ever retreating.

On the third day they saw the first trading post. The tiny log structure, backed by a crude barn and corrals, sprang unexpectedly into view beside a stream and cluster of trees. Contrasted with the days of bleak travel, it was more than civilization. Poor though it was, it was comfort and warmth in contrast to the nights of cold when they had slept sheltered by animal skins and curled around their tiny fire.

Joshua pulled his horse ahead of them. "I'll see if they'll have us for the night." They trailed slowly after him, watching him dismount and stride toward the building.

As Rebecca reluctantly followed, she was realizing that this was the first cabin she had seen since leaving Cedar City. The sight of the log structure threw fearful memories at her.

A fat man in greasy buckskins stood in the doorway listening to Joshua. Spitting a stream of tobacco juice and shifting the plug in his mouth, he said, "Don't 'low no Injuns in the place. If'n you buddy with them, you and yer little fella can sleep in the barn with 'em."

Rebecca's quick intake of breath occasioned a hard, quick glance from Joshua before he said, "That's not right charitable."

" 'Tis." The man smote the doorjamb with his clenched fist.

"I aim to be friendly. Ain't I trustin' 'em Redskins with my horses?"

Rebecca was sputtering with righteous indignation as Joshua hurried them out to the barn. There was a touch of amusement in Solali's eyes as she ran after Rebecca. "Never you mind. 'Tis common what he's saying. We hear it often." The amusement turned to tenderness. " 'Tis good to see you ruffle your feathers like a sage hen."

The following day they traveled into a snowstorm. Although the storm started with light flakes merely veiling the rolling hills and clumps of sage, the wind rose and whipped the snow into hedges of misery. They spent the day struggling through drifts that blanketed their legs in bone-chilling cold.

As the afternoon passed slowly, Rebecca knew she had reached her limit of endurance. Her numb hands could no longer master the pony, and she clung to her rabbit-skin robe and wished for her misery to end.

She was beyond caring when the trail broadened into a road and they were curving westward. When there were trees and corrals snugged beside a long adobe building, her pony stopped beside the others.

Briefly she was aware of Joshua's blue eyes heavy with concern. There were his arms to lift her down. Later she remembered the shock of his warmth, the thud of his heart, and the bite of a cold circle pressing against her cheek. Now she knew only Solali's poking, whispering, guiding and pushing.

There was a rush mattress, and the two of them collapsed together while strange hands stripped snow-encrusted garments from them. Hot liquid was pressed to their lips, and then the blessed quietness of sleep.

When Rebecca was next aware of Joshua, he was bending close, speaking while his anxious eyes studied her face. "Becka," he said urgently, "we won't be leaving. They'll let us stay until the snow is gone. You are safe. There's nothing to harm you here."

"When you call me 'Becka' you sound like Jamie," she murmured. She reached, trying to touch him with a hand which was stone heavy.

"We'll see Jamie soon, just as soon as the willows are green and the water runs free. Rebecca, the worst is over. The fearsome things are gone. Please, just get well—strong." The urgency of his concern for her made her gaze into his shadowed face. Seeing the lines of weariness again, she wondered what she had said during those bad hours.

The way station to which the group had come during the snowstorm was on the Goose Creek Trail, the main east-west emigrant trail crossing Utah Territory into California. They were told it was an extension of the Central Overland Trail between St. Louis and Salt Lake City. On this trail goods were carried to the mines in California, while mail and passengers traveled eastward. During the winter months it was used chiefly by freighters moving their ponderous wagons north and south, east and west.

While the spring storms continued to pile snow along the route, the flow of travelers continued. Rebecca and Solali quickly found themselves pressed into service, and the adobe way station seemed to expand and contract with people. Lonely, defeated miners trickled eastward; brawny freighters, cheered by their own success, moved westward.

Life centered around the yawning fireplace in the main room. The plank tables beside the fire were laden with the freighters' beans and flour, transformed into hearty meals by Rebecca and Solali. They carried steaming pots of stew and platters of venison while they listened to the men talk.

Discouraged miners lifted their foaming tankards while the freighters lifted their voices. "You mark my words. In a couple a' years there'll be stagecoaches crossin' this land ever' day. There'll be folks movin' faster'n they ever moved before. And it won't just be the miners. This country is a curious place to them back east. Folks all just waitin' to visit the wild west. There's fellas achin' to shoot themselves a buffalo, and ladies dyin' to see what a plural wife looks like and whether Brigham Young has two heads."

There was news. The gold fields in California were about exhausted, but there was talk of gold in Oregon. Rebecca's eyes sought Joshua's, remembering the letters from his youth. Those letters had been filled with hope and then despair. Would he be tempted again by the tantalizing tales? His blue eyes answered with a steady gaze which told her nothing.

The weeks passed. Between snowstorms they could see the hills were greening, and the trees, too, were fluffed with a cloud of green.

While Joshua and Eagle paced restlessly between the inn and the corrals, waiting for the storms to cease, Rebecca was discovering the blessing of this new interlude. With the constant pressure of hungry men to be fed, she was being pressed into service each day with just one more task than it seemed her strength would allow. But through the fatigue she was feeling a new challenge. When she wanted nothing more than surcease, there was one more task. And then there were Joshua's eyes.

In the beginning, when she had first taken over the task of baking bread, while she handled the dough with clumsy hands, attempting to spare the tortured muscles on her wounded side, Joshua had watched her. She had seen him and recognized when his lips whitened in response to the pain she couldn't conceal. In these days she felt the tiny nudge of that old spirited Rebecca who would not be beholden to anyone. She forced her smile and gritted her teeth. It was a glad surprise when she discovered the agony paid in dividends of strength and new freedom from pain.

Late one evening she was alone, resting beside the fire in the main room of the inn. The guests had moved to their rooms, and she was nodding in her cozy spot when Joshua came through the room, hesitated, then joined her.

She listened to the quiet rumble of his voice for a while and then with a yawn said, "That's a patter of nothing talk; why aren't you going to bed like the others?" She rubbed her heavy eyes and peered at him.

"And why aren't you?"

"Guess I'm too tired to face the task of getting there."

Abruptly he squatted beside her and lifted her right arm. She winced as he straightened the arm and lifted it, forcing it past the stretching pain. Now he folded it back into her lap.

"Where were you injured?" he asked softly as his eyes continued to search her face.

Silently she raised her left hand and drew a line extending down her right side from under her arm to the edge of her ribs. "It—I must have moved because it was only a flesh wound."

" 'Must have moved'—dear God!" he murmured. She watched his eyes darken. Abruptly he got to his feet and left the room.

CHAPTER 3

It was March when the lone rider came in from Great Salt Lake City. That night the stranger was the only guest, and he was full of talk as he sat at the long table between Joshua and the proprietor of the station, Hank Walker.

Rebecca studied the man as she listened. He was marked with a great weariness, but his clothing and gear indicated he was not one of the defeated ones. Obviously he was a traveler with a purpose. When asked about his destination he showed a hint of bitterness. "California."

"Why didn't you wait for the weather to break?" Hank asked.

"I'd had all of Utah I could stomach." He turned to Joshua. "You said you'd be traveling on in a few weeks. Don't take that cut going through the City of Rocks. You'll never make it."

"Why, what's going on?" Joshua asked in surprise.

"Highwaymen. They hole up in a hideout on Goose Creek. A little bunch like yours would be easy pickings."

Joshua studied the man before asking, "You had trouble?"

"No. I'd been warned by those who had. I'm just passing the word along. Seems the best way."

"Obliged, but we're heading the other direction."

"Well, it's a good thing. You know there's bound to be more trouble in Utah Territory. Washington's sent spies up the Colorado. They wouldn't do that unless they had something serious up their sleeves. The Saints are just too big a handful for Washington."

"What makes you think they're spies?" Walker asked.

"Everybody is saying. Besides, what else'd they be? Amasa Lyman thinks a big attack is planned for up the river. He's sent word to Brigham, and now he's at Cedar organizing men. There's rumor he's planning to look for a place to hole up over in the Pyramid Canyon area. I hear tell they're going to call the missionaries and settlers in from all over, places like Las Vegas."

Joshua stabbed at the venison on his plate. "Is Young still planning on moving his people south?"

"You'd better believe he is! President Buchanan's trying to bring in a Gentile governor along with the troops. They're determined to keep peace and make a good little Territory out a' Utah. Brigham Young is just as determined that he'll conquer. He's got a thousand fighting men ready to go." The man stopped to take a big swallow of hot coffee before continuing.

"Last fall, just before I got to the Territory, ol' Brig preached a sermon that set the people back on their heels. He made no bones about how he saw the whole situation. He said that he would be President of the United States, Heber C. Kimball would be Vice-President, and Brother Wells, Secretary of the Interior. But until that came about, the Saints would go to hell, just as surely as they stood there listening to him, if they ever deposed him as governor." He returned to his supper.

Curiously Rebecca watched Joshua. He seemed to be having trouble controlling his feelings. Finally he asked, "How do the people feel about all this?"

"They're behind him; leastwise, he's outfitted men with money from the tithing office. Seems like approval to me. They say they're ready for action right now."

Later Solali detained Joshua with a timid hand on his sleeve. They paused to watch Rebecca carry the empty platters into the kitchen; then Solali whispered, "Do you see it? The Saints will be coming this way. They must—there's no other place to run."

Joshua turned and paced restlessly to the fireplace. On his second trip he stopped to kick at a protruding log. "Solali," he said, "I nearly killed her getting her this far. I'm afraid to move on."

"I know what you heard and saw when the fever came up,"

Solali said, "But now there's new strength in her."

He nodded. "I know. I've watched her forcing her body, making it gain strength. I know it hasn't been easy. But that journey was so bad, I'm fearful. I can't risk more right now." He stopped and cleared his throat. The haunted eyes of Rebecca never ceased overlapping his memory of a laughing, happy girl.

"She's like a wounded bird," Solali whispered, "but she will fly again. When the sun breaks through and the air is soft, just watch her spirit soar."

"Please, God," he whispered. "But until that day—"

It was the middle of March now. While the sun brightened and warmed the earth, the wind softened, but Joshua lingered on. And while he was lingering, the wagon train arrived.

When the three wagons pulled by weary, overloaded oxen crept into the station, Joshua had been watching them for an hour. They were coming down the trail from the west—that should have settled his worries. When he saw the load of household goods bulging from the wagon, he decided the occupants were gold miners returning east. As soon as the woman climbed down, carrying a crying infant and shooing the toddler before her, he went to help with the teams.

Rebecca was in the kitchen when she heard the infant cry. With a puzzled frown she turned to Solali. "A wagon train just came in," Solali murmured as she continued to stir the simmering stew.

The baby was newborn. Rebecca settled the woman in a rocking chair close to the cookstove, then hovered over the pair with painful fascination.

Solali came in with a piece of bread for the wide-eyed boy while the infant began to nurse. The young woman sighed and leaned back in the chair. "Aw, it's good to have the world quit movin' for a time. I'm Katie Martin. We've come from Genoa. Movin' back to the Territory." She settled herself more comfortably. "This is a new place. Weren't nothin' 'long this stretch three years ago when we moved to Genoa."

Abruptly Solali spoke, "Genoa. Used to be called Mormon Station, didn't it? It's over Pyramid Mountain area, isn't it?"

The woman nodded. "You're Indian, but you surely do speak

good English." She said nothing more, but when Rebecca turned from the stove, she saw her intently studying Solali. There was a slight frown on her face, but she asked no questions.

Briskly Rebecca said, "These biscuits are done. Suppose we start serving the menfolk now." She ducked her head toward Katie. "You stay if you wish and we'll get things going out there."

"My husband will be a'wonderin' what's become of me."

"I'll tell him." Rebecca picked up the platter of meat and followed Solali into the big room.

Rebecca placed the platter on the table and Solali rapped a tin cup against a plate to signal dinner.

"Miss?" The man's voice questioned behind her.

"Oh, yes, I was to tell you—" with a smile Rebecca turned. She caught her breath and backed against the table, trying desperately to hang on to her composure.

The eldest son of Bishop Martin stared at her. "I know you, don't I? Wasn't it, ah—"

"Your wife—" Rebecca hastily interrupted, "she's with the young'uns in the kitchen. She says eat with the men. She'll—"

"Oh, yes," he smiled, and then the puzzled look returned. "I know you from somewhere, don't I?"

She dared not remind him of Cedar City, of Andrew, of her old school just outside the fort. But, then, he had been her student only a brief time before his long legs and restless energy had carried him on his way. Genoa—Mormon Station it had been. Why hadn't she remembered he had been sent there? The silence was lengthening.

"Why," she said slowly, "seems I always remind folks of the last towhead they knew." With a shrug he settled himself at the table and she sighed with relief.

Passing to and fro throughout the evening, carrying the loaded platters and returning the empty ones, Rebecca once again found Steven Martin's puzzled frown following her.

Later she saw the measuring glance that moved between her blondness and Joshua's. As she walked away from the table, she heard him ask Joshua. "Where you headed—California?"

She waited in the doorway, holding her breath and desperately willing Joshua to silence. But there was his answer, "No. Oregon. I have a place in the Willamette Valley, up near where the Willamette and the McKenzie rivers join."

"Been there long?"

"Long enough to get me a good piece of land in the richest farming country you've ever seen."

Hank Walker, curious, was watching Rebecca. Quickly she moved to take his empty plate and return to the room with the coffeepot.

Joshua had been watching Rebecca, too. When her hand had trembled against his coffee cup, he had wondered. As Rebecca returned to the kitchen, Katie Martin came into the room and spoke to her husband.

He got to his feet. "I'll go check on Sanders and the team. Let him get some supper."

After a moment, Joshua picked up his coffee cup and headed for the kitchen. "More of that Java?" he inquired, sticking his head around the doorjamb.

Rebecca was bent over the dishpan and merely nodded. Solali lifted the pot, murmuring, "I think Eagle's come back. I thought I saw him through the window."

"I'll mosey out to the corrals," Joshua said. He drained the cup and slipped it into the dishpan. Crossing the kitchen, he let himself out the back door. The light from the window laid a rectangular path of brightness pointing the direction to the corral. He started down the path and felt a detaining hand on his arm.

It was Eagle. A quick hand touched his lips and a tug took him off the path and against the side of the barn. Eagle's hand still held him silent. There was a conversation taking place on the other side of the wall and words drifted through.

Joshua moved impatiently. The men were talking about moving east, not west. Now a word caught his attention. *Towhead.* He heard, "She wouldn't admit she recognized me, and that makes me wonder. I'll bet you fifty she's Andrew Jacobson's wife. Can't help thinkin' he'd like to know that."

Joshua's chest ached with the pain of holding his breath.

Eagle's hand guided him away from the wall. They circled the inn and stopped. Eagle's face was grim. "Pinto, Cedar men."

Joshua was beginning to get himself under control. He took a deep breath. "So you recognized them. I'm guessing it isn't a good idea to stick around here any longer." He clasped the shoulder of the Indian and said, "Go to the kitchen and get some grub in you and give me a chance to think about this."

Rebecca heard the light tap on the door. With her hands still submerged in suds, she watched Solali open the door and stand aside. Eagle spoke to Solali in Paiute, his words urgent and low.

Solali went to fill a plate for him. "He's been to the Indian villages south of here and says there's a bad feeling. It's because Brigham's made promises he can't keep."

"How's that?"

"Like being a battle-axe of the Lord—that means no Indian will be killed while he's fighting for Brigham Young. We know that isn't so, and the Indians are murmuring against the white men now. Also they are being forced deeper into the desert where there's nothing to feed their families."

Eagle finished his supper and went into the main room of the inn. Rebecca hung her towels and watched Solali go to their tiny room behind the stairs. Through the doorway she could see Eagle and Joshua still standing beside the fireplace.

Nighttime sounds were claiming the inn. Overhead the floor timbers creaked and a child whimpered.

The voices beside the fire dropped, and the flames crackled as the backlog was positioned for the night. The stairs creaked again. From her station by the door, Rebecca could see that Joshua stood alone. Still wondering what she should tell him about the Martins, she slipped out to stand beside him.

Now she saw that he was holding a black-bound book. "Ah," she whispered, "is that the Bible you bought in California?"

He nodded and pulled a bench close to the fire. "Lately I've not spent much time with it, searching out what it has to say."

"Do you think that's important?"

"Becky, I'm knowin' the Lord's approval every time I open the pages, but more, I'm knowin' it's a real guiding hand."

She sat down beside him and plucked at the threadbare calico she wore. "Seems I'm losing my hankering for it. I was trying to live up to it for a long time, but lately my faith's like this old dress—about to give out on me."

"Are you back to thinkin' you have to earn the blessings of the Lord?" he asked.

Her head snapped up and she looked at him. "That's the way it appears, doesn't it? I guess I've been watching the ground for so long I'm afraid to look up."

"You've been sick and weak. Now—" his voice faltered and she glanced at him, surprised to catch the frown, the lines pressing his lips hard. Unexpectedly a tiny hard knot in her heart loosened.

She whispered, "Joshua, you've been such a wonderful friend. How can I ever repay you?"

There was only silence. She watched his hands tighten on the Book. Finally he fumbled with the pages and his voice was low. As he read to her, she became conscious of the center of her being becoming tender, sore. He was repeating words that had been familiar and dear to her the previous year. But now they were making her realize there was a threat within her. It seemed the words were trying to break down a wall she had built, stone by stone.

She jumped to her feet. Pressing her hand against her throat she whispered, " 'He's come to give me life,' 'trust in the Father,' 'trust in Him.' Joshua, right now I'm fearful to listen to the words. Someday—" She brushed past him and rushed to the kitchen.

"Rebecca." She stood waiting with her back to him. Out of the silence he spoke in an even voice. "I'm sorry. I don't understand. One of these days when you feel like talking your heart feelings, I'd be glad to listen."

But Rebecca was busy remembering the words he had read. The thoughts circled through her mind, demanding an entrance deep inside, but she wanted only to shut out the words. Yet they were there and they couldn't be denied. She pressed her hands against her cold cheeks.

Now more words were coming into her mind. " 'I will not

leave you comfortless . . . my peace I give unto you . . . ' " Such words couldn't be ignored; they must be accepted or disproved. But there was another thing she was seeing for the first time: Jesus' words had become Joshua's words. She looked at him uneasily, wondering how she had missed that before and what it would mean now.

Suddenly he spoke urgently. "Rebecca, we must go. Tomorrow. I'm sorry, but it must be." He turned and took the stairs two at a time. Astonished, she watched him. Now she was realizing that she hadn't told him about Steven Martin. For a moment she hesitated and then shrugged. No matter. They would soon be gone and it wouldn't be important. After tomorrow it would not be a thing to fret about.

CHAPTER 4

It was good to be back on the road—even Rebecca was feeling it. They were moving away from Utah Territory and steadily working their way toward Oregon.

At times the road before them seemed to inch along through the sand and barren bush. The mountains circled around them, remote, with only a dreamlike promise of a fairer land beyond them.

Once again the snow swirled about them, as if the Territory were reluctant to release them without a final thrust of misery. Again the horses walked slowly, bowing their heads to the storm as the people on their backs huddled in misery. But the way stations were clustered along the length of the California trail, and each night they were able to find shelter.

On the day that the sun shone brightly again and the snow disappeared, Joshua said, "Today we'll be headin' north. The Applegate trail is just ahead."

"Applegate," Rebecca repeated dully.

"Or Old South Road as it's known back home," Joshua explained. " 'Twas cut through soon after the terrible trips in '44 and '45 down the Columbia. The Applegates lost a couple of children when they were shipping down the river. The rapids just about make the trip impossible."

"I don't understand," Solali said. "We've heard about the Oregon Trail; what's this road?"

"The Oregon Trail cuts straight north through the Territory. From Fort Boise, where we were, the trail jogs west first and then north, clear to the river."

"The Columbia?" Rebecca questioned, sitting straighter in the saddle now.

"Yes, then it goes west only to The Dalles."

"If the rapids on the river are so bad, why don't they cut a trail?"

"There's no place to hang it on those bluffs," Joshua said ruefully. "Portage is so bad there'd be a road down the river if it were in man's power to build one."

He continued, "There's the pass through the Cascade Mountains now. Barlow cut it through in '45. It's south out of The Dalles and goes west over the mountains. The Applegate road joins with it in the valley. In the beginning the Old South Road was cut to give better access to the Willamette Valley. That's enough—we've only one road to contend with now. Right soon we'll ride up north across the end of California and drop down through the mountains into Oregon."

He was quiet for a long time. Finally he spoke again, reluctantly. "This next section of road cuts through lava beds and mighty thirsty land before it reaches Oregon. We've had a heap of Indian trouble along the road 'til '56. But then, I guess, we'd really been askin' for it ever since the land was settled." He paused to slant an apologetic glance at Solali and Eagle.

"Guess hindsight is better than foresight," he commented. "Leastwise, now we can see where we've gone wrong. That is," he qualified, "some of us are seein' and wonderin' how to rectify the situation." He turned to study Rebecca's face. "Pushing the tribes out of their homes doesn't make more sense than their pushing back. Don't you forget, Oregon's just as raw as Utah. Maybe our troubles are a shade easier to handle, but they still need settlin'. You'll not expect a heaven on earth, I hope."

She lifted her head and frowned at him. "I reckon I'd not given it much thought. You're saying there's scrapping to be done before things are settled. I recall your letters lent that air."

"Then you remember about the Whitmans?" He waited for her nod before adding. "They're the doctor and his wife murdered by the Indians. Well, from that time on till last year, '56, there's been trouble."

"That's been nearly ten years." Her voice was low as she tried to hide the dismay rising in her heart. She closed her eyes briefly against the dark thoughts.

As if guessing, he hurried on, "You've got to understand the situation. For the Whitmans, the climax came when the Indians around their mission were hit by a measles epidemic. 'Twas bad enough on the white man, but they'd been hardened to such disease. The red man hasn't. The whole lot of Indians demanded Whitman cure their disease, and when he couldn't, they saw it as conspiracy since the white men were recovering. To compound the problem, the red man took to his steam house to try his own cure. That made matters worse."

They rode in silence as Rebecca recalled the story Joshua had written in one of his letters. After years of ministering to the Indians, the doctor and his wife were murdered in their home. Before the end, others had died also.

"Like I said," he murmured, "hindsight. If we'd just learn to respect their ways, let them live like always, we could've been neighbors, peaceable."

Joshua was quiet for a long time and then he chuckled and shook his head. "There was one good story that came out of the mess about an Indian who refused to take part in the killings. Seems maybe the Whitmans did manage to convert one Indian. I heard this story old Joel Palmer told on himself. Said he met an Indian chief and the fellow asked him if he was a Christian. Old Palmer said yes, and that seemed to be the end of the matter until the chief caught him playin' cards. Joel said by the time the chief finished with him, his jaw was hanging to his knees. This supposedly wild and unlearned savage, twenty-five hundred miles from civilization, was tellin' him how to live right before the Lord. Made quite an impression, and Palmer determined he'd leave the card playin' alone forever." His voice dropped to a musing note. "Imagine, one Indian completely converted. A totally changed life. Proves it can happen." Rebecca wondered at the note of awe in his voice.

The next day as they walked their horses up a rocky cut, Rebecca asked, "What's Oregon like?"

"Like everything you've ever seen. Green and fertile with

rolling hills like Illinois. Barren in spots like the desert we've ridden. I've traveled the Oregon Trail from one end to the other twice now. I've been down California way and crossed back to Utah Territory three times now. But it's Oregon for me."

Rebecca pondered his words. She knew of the times he had entered Utah Territory looking for her. *What if* . . . Suppose he had found her on that first trip? She knew a moment of bitterness as she forced her thoughts away from those shadowy pictures her mind threw at her. Still, *what if*?

His words cutting through her thoughts were gentle now. Perhaps he too was handling the *what ifs*. "The Willamette Valley where Pa and I have taken land is as fair a place as you could ask for."

He slanted an easy grin at her. "The Donation Land Act Congress passed in 1850 gives every man 320 acres. If he has a wife, she gets 320 acres too. Pa and I had a nice piece of the valley, snugged up together with plenty of water. It's rollin' hills backed by timbered acres. Just back of it all, the mountains rear pretty sharp-like. There's neighbors, but even Pa can wiggle his elbows without gettin' them in somebody's soup."

Later as they rode their horses across the corner of California, he said, "There's trees and rivers and mountains. And fir marches right up the side of the mountain. There's lumber for houses and pasture for livestock. There's soil achin' for the plow and there's room for everybody who wants to come, and for the passel of young'uns he'll raise.

"Down Salem way you can hear the sawmills screechin' and the riverboats tootin'. That's progress. Matt's farming down there now. It's wheat country, and they're shipping it out fast as they can raise it." For a while he was busy with his own thoughts; then, "Salem's the capital of the Territory now. Things are rolling there. It you want to see action, you go to Salem."

Again he slumped in the saddle, his voice dreamy. "Oregon's a right pretty place. When the woodsmoke curls around through the wet trees, a log cabin feels mighty good. Makes a man feel snug and warm, right at home. You plant wheat in the autumn and sit and wait for the winter rains to nourish it along. Come summer you cut the wheat, thresh the grain, grind it into flour.

Then you put it on a ship and send it to California. We exchange our gold for theirs. But we'll never run out like they will. We don't dig it, we plant it."

Rebecca's mind ran on with his words, drawing mental pictures of her own. She was replacing, transplanting the old with the promise of new. His words seemed to make a spell, enticing and luring her on. She could almost forget the shadows of the past.

Now he straightened in the saddle. Ahead of them were the mountains, drifting blue-green with the misty rain. They climbed through gentle air soft with the wind-borne scents of Oregon. Still dreamy with Joshua's talk, Rebecca thought she was catching a scent of Salem's woodsmoke in the midst of the pine.

Here in the mountains she was seeing moss growing thick on the north side of the delicate trees, woven into a mist of fairy lace. Was that trunk a spindle resting against the sky?

On the day the mountain began to slant downward, Joshua grinned at her and said, "Becky, welcome to Oregon Territory. You're home."

Home! She turned away to hide the tears. The word slashed through the hardened dreams and splintered fences she had gathered to hide her soul.

They rounded that last sharp promontory, and Oregon rolled gently out before her like folds of green velvet. Joshua was watching her. After her first stunned surprise, she moved, looking about with delight. "This is Oregon." It wasn't a question; she was affirming it. She was accepting it with a stirring of senses she thought had been gone forever.

As Solali's horse grazed her way even with Rebecca, the Indian woman studied first the scenery and then Rebecca's face. "It's like a picture book, isn't it?" she whispered. "Like as if you turn the page, it's gone." A shadow touched her face and Rebecca wondered at the sadness.

Hastily Joshua said, "But this picture won't disappear; it'll be better. Welcome to the fairest section of the country. Oregon Territory, soon to become a state."

Rebecca's indrawn breath was ragged, nearly tearful, and

Joshua's voice deepened as he expressed what now could be pulled out of the back of their thoughts and faced. "Just as sure as we rode out of that Territory and lived to tell it, we've come into new life. It's different here, Rebecca. The past is over forever; you can forget it now."

The silence of the peaceful land seemed to flow into them and they lingered. It was Joshua who moved first. He pushed his dusty hat away from his face. Rebecca turned to face him.

"You say it's over, that this is all new life." Her voice was low. For a moment she couldn't bring her eyes up to meet Joshua's, but when she did, forcing a brave smile, she pleaded, "Please, may it really be so?" Across the space that separated them she saw him frown. "Joshua, may I bind you to secrecy?" Now her voice was cold, hard, as she said, "My past must never be mentioned again if I am truly to live a new life."

"You know Ma and Pa'll find that hard." Joshua would have much rather promised her the silence she requested. But he went on, "They know where you've been; don't they have a right to know?" Shaking her head, she pressed her lips and reached for the reins. He stretched a staying hand. "Becky, I'm still not touching the real girl, am I? I'm sorry." He was shaking his head. As he turned his horse, he said, "I'm feelin' this way deep down inside of me. Becky, this secret is wrong. It's a mistake." But to her retreating back he said, "I'll respect your wishes."

He moved ahead and led the way down the mountain to the green valley. When the rocks were behind them and they rode side by side through the meadows, Joshua said, "We've still a fair piece before we reach home. We'll head up Jacksonville way for now. I want to see Scotty MacLennan. I've heard scarce a word about the Territory since I've been gone."

"Is Jacksonville a goodly town?" Solali asked.

"Fair. They've been mining for gold hereabouts since '51. Here and the Josephine."

"You have?" Rebecca's quick question drew a glance from him, and Eagle turned to look at them.

"Nope. I recovered from my spot of gold fever right sharp and haven't been drawn since. Didn't take much gawkin' over the top of the dredge to convince me that the ladies doing the laundry were richer than we were. No mining for me; I'll take my riches the hard way."

The day was far spent when they turned west to follow the creek along the edge of the mountain. Joshua let his horse mosey along until Rebecca caught up with him. She noticed the taut lines on his face had relaxed into a pleasant half-grin.

"It's good to be back, to be free to settle in and start livin'." Shooting a quick look her way he said, "I'm not complaining about the past; I'm trying to explain how I feel now."

"Joshua"—she could only bring her voice up to a whisper— "I'll never be forgetting how you've put yourself out just for me. I'm guessing you've never half settled in here because of me and that land would be nearly fallow if it weren't for your folks and Jamie."

He nodded, adding, "We're not wanting you to feel beholdin', not a one of us. I've explained why I've gone lookin'. It was a need bigger than myself. The need's satisfied now. No matter how you make your life from here on in, the need's satisfied; that satisfies me." His glance slid sideways as if gauging her response. With a sigh she accepted this newest gift. He was holding her in an easy grip, not demanding.

Now a startling thought made her straighten in the saddle. If the grip was loosening, could it mean he no longer wanted her? What about those letters? Were they merely a part of the past that must be forgotten? Those promises were only the promises of youth. She looked down at her hands; ragged, weathered and well-used, they belonged to a different Rebecca. The woman riding beside this Joshua was not the girl he had left in Illinois.

"We've been through a bad place in the road together," he said softly. "But that's no reason to keep you beholden to me for the rest of your life. I sure don't want it that way."

He settled his hat against the slanting rays of the sun and continued, "Life's a hard enough patch to hoe without havin' the blamed rocks in the way."

Later, when they were entering the outskirts of Jacksonville, Rebecca realized their journey along the cabin-spiked trail hadn't prepared her for this. Her mind was still filled with the memory of log cabins guarded by squawking chickens and spotted bovines as they rode through Jacksonville's tree-lined streets. White picket fences and milled lumber houses painted white and pooled in brilliant flower gardens marked their way.

The hitching post where Joshua tied her horse belonged to the white clapboard house. Its wide verandas were bedecked with wicker furniture and scarlet geraniums in clay pots.

"Joshua, I can't," Rebecca whispered. "Not dressed like this, I can't." She touched her trail-stained buckskin pants and shrank back.

"This isn't the governor's mansion. This is just Scotty's." He was still wearing that pleased grin.

Slowly she followed Joshua's eager strides. "Scott!" he bellowed, heading around the house toward the barn. With a crash and a cloud of dust, the barn door banged against the building.

Rebecca was still watching the dust rise and the wall vibrate when the man burst through the door with a shout of glee. Towering above them, wearing clothing as tattered and stained as theirs, carrying a pitchfork, he rubbed his tousled red hair and roared, "Joshua, me lad! You've returned to the promised land. And have ye settled your brothers so's that you ken claim your inheritance?" He thumped Joshua's shoulder and wheeled around. "Aw, a fair one you've brought, and these are your Indian friends." Even Eagle's face relaxed as the Scotsman pumped his hand.

They settled on the veranda and drank buttermilk frosted with coolness. When the sun had dipped behind the last hill and Rebecca's teeth began to chatter, she was rescued by an Indian woman and swooped into the kitchen for hot tea. Scotty's introductions trailed after them. This was his wife, Matilda.

There was no time to explain—the chatters were more nerves than cold. In the kitchen she was immediately surrounded. She saw two more dusky-hued women and a dark-eyed child. As Rebecca was settled in a chair beside the cookstove, the women were introduced. The child was Ross and his mother was Star, Matilda's sister. Tika was her friend, and all three were from the Klamath tribe.

Scotty had come into the kitchen to introduce the women.

With his arm about Matilda, he addressed Solali. "I suppose you'll be able to talk their lingo. Seems no matter what tribe, you manage to understand each other."

Matilda, dressed in a demure calico dress with a spotless white apron, wore her lustrous hair coiled against her neck in a decidedly un-Indian fashion. She spoke with a gentle Scottish burr. "It is the tie of blood and earth, not language, because there is a difference." She patted his arm and gave him a gentle push toward the door. "Now, off with those muddy boots if you're to set one foot beyond this kitchen."

CHAPTER 5

While the woman heaped the serving platters, Scotty waved his guests toward the door across the kitchen. Matilda led the way into the dining room.

Rebecca's eyes took in a table, round and bedecked with snowy white to match their hostess' apron. The plates and platters were china—matching china. "This is Oregon Territory," she murmured in a wondering voice. "I'd guess me back east, not the farthest end of civilization."

They finished the venison roast and the fried chicken with the heaps of garden vegetables. There had been tender light bread and delicate preserves too.

Big wedges of dried apple pie were being pushed across the table before Rebecca could take her eyes off the marvel of the room. She poked her fork into the pie. These people and their homes were telling a story far more clearly than words. And the story was a sharp contrast to all Rebecca had known before.

She looked at the shiny, dark sideboard. The brilliant mirror above it reflected the sparkle of crystal and the glow of lamplight. These people were part of a community that was well established, secure. There was money enough for houses, which were more than mere crude shelters against bullets, fire, and weather.

She found herself acknowledging it all with a slight nodding of her head. *People don't import fancy furniture like this if they're wondering whether the Indians will leave it alone,* she mused. *You don't have china and crystal if your stomach is gnawing*

44

from poor and scanty victuals. And, furthermore, she noted that a carpet like the one under her feet wasn't designed for muddy boots. Yet Scotty looked like he could have been transported from Utah.

With a start, Rebecca became aware of the conversation tossed back and forth between Joshua and Scotty. She glanced at Joshua and saw the yearning on his face. She turned to Scotty, wondering at his power to bring out that expression. The red-haired giant was hunched across the table, rumbling the china and silver as his fist punctuated each phrase with a thump on the table.

"Scotty," Joshua answered, "quit guiltin' me with leaving the Territory last August just before the constitutional convention. Just tell me what I missed. You knew I couldn't wait forever! I explained—" He hesitated and quickly glanced at Rebecca.

Scotty nodded and said, "Well, first off, you know as well as I do that circumstances made it so as everything pointed to stoppin' the squabbling and gettin' with it to become a state. The squabbling's been going on since '56, so you know all about it."

"It's about like two brothers scrapping."

"Right. It goes on and on, with matters just gettin' worse. But let an outsider stick his neck in and—"

"That's all it takes to get things settled in a hurry. Differences don't matter anymore."

"On our part," Scotty murmured contentedly, "the Dred Scott decision was a blessing. Leastways, it finally spurred us on to get with the issue of becoming a state."

"Dred Scott," Rebecca ventured timidly, "does that have anything to do with you?"

"Naw, he's no kinfolk of mine." Scotty was laughing now. "I came by my name through the back door. Weren't born with it."

"It's a handle," Joshua explained. "He's a native-born son of Scotland. The hair and the brogue stuck before his name did. Scotty's easier to remember than MacLennan."

"Dred Scott," Scotty came back to her question, "was a black man, trying to gain his freedom in a legal way. He said since he'd lived in a free state, he was free."

"Free state," Rebecca repeated. "That's one that didn't hold with having slaves?"

He nodded. "The country's been fightin' this thing since Thomas Jefferson's time. Mark my words, the rumbling's gettin' worse. There's going to be big trouble before the issue's settled." He stopped and sighed. Now facing Rebecca he explained, "When this all started the Union had settled on something they called the Missouri Compromise."

"I've heard about it," Rebecca said. "But the Dred Scott thing, what is that?"

"Happened about a year ago." Scotty settled back in his chair. "The decision. Dred Scott was a slave belonging to a Dr. Emerson, an army surgeon. In the progress of moving about, Scott was forced to spend two years in a non-slave state. Later he was returned to Missouri and his master died. Then he sued for freedom, sayin' that his living in a non-slave state actually made him a free man. Well, there was some shenanigans that went on, desperate man that he was, but finally his case reached the Supreme Court. The gist of the ruling handed down said that Negroes couldn't be citizens, the Missouri Compromise was unconstitutional, and Congress had no power to restrict slavery in the territories.

Rebecca pondered, trying to understand. Finally she spoke. "I know the Missouri Compromise sets limits on which states could be slave states, and says the northern part of the Louisiana Purchase would be free."

"At the time," Joshua explained, "this meant there would be twelve slave states and twelve free. Also it denied Congress the right to set restrictions on slavery in new territories seeking admission to the Union."

"But it was repealed by the Kansas-Nebraska Act," Scotty reminded them. "The part we're most concerned about's called 'popular sovereignty.' This is meanin' that the territories have the right to decide whether or not they will allow slavery in their states. At the time of admission, their constitution's to be written for or against slavery."

"And this is affecting Oregon?"

"The Territorial Constitution said no slavery. The Dred Scott Act said Congress had no right to restrict slavery in the territories. This was our chance. The blamed Territory has been draggin' its heels for years. Now was the time to settle down and get some serious business done."

Scotty paused to laugh gleefully. "I'll tell you, things have been hot around here ever since! Washington rumbles had it that Oregon would be another slave state. True, there were plenty casting their votes that way, and since then there's been many secessionist ideas circulated. But we fooled them all!

"In the end, when we got around to votin' on the constitution as a whole, there were only three items on the ballot for ratification. They were: do ya vote for the constitution, do ya vote for slavery in Oregon, and do ya vote for free Negroes?"

"Lane's the Territorial delegate to Congress, and he's soft for the South," Joshua warned.

"And he's bound he'll be the state's first senator." Scotty sat up straight and shook his finger at Joshua. "Josh, me lad, you need to start pushin' right now."

Joshua was shaking his head. "I'm too young."

"Oregon's young. Your next protest is that you're only a frontiersman. Everybody in the Territory falls in the same cast. Not a one of the bunch is a professional statesman. You stand as good a chance as the next man."

Rebecca's head was whirling from pivoting back and forth between the two men. She heard Joshua's protest again and Scotty's retort, "A man can't hold back for any feeble excuse, or we'll lose the state to the pro-slavery forces."

"You're puttin' the pressure on me."

"And I will until I'm assured you'll be at the Republican Convention." He paused for a moment and then added. "Wouldn't hurt you a mite to become a Republican."

"I've no choice," Joshua stated bluntly. "The Democratic party is splittin' apart over slavery."

During the conversation, Matilda motioned to Star and Tika. The two rose and began to clear the table. Solali joined them.

When the table had been emptied down to the snowy cloth, Tika closed the kitchen door.

Scotty shoved his chair closer to Rebecca and rested his arms on the table. "My dear Miss Rebecca, if you're going to be a part of this new place, it's important you understand all of this."

With a mock reproving glance at Joshua, he added, "I can't imagine why you've failed to acquaint the young lady with the goings on in the Territory. I'm guessin' you thought you had better things to talk about. But there'll be no harboring an ignorant one here. Every man and woman in the Territory has got to come and settle himself down to being concerned about it all."

"But slavery?" Rebecca questioned. "Law, I'd heard it was dying out."

"Well, it ain't. It's a device of the devil himself to pass the rumors that make a man complacent."

Matilda stirred and stretched a gentle hand toward her husband. Rebecca still marveled at the soft burr coming from the Indian lips. "Scotty, it can't be *all* politics. Miss Rebecca will be fearin' that's all we are—politicians."

She turned to Rebecca. "You know we have a stagecoach comin' most days, least when the mud's not hub deep. It travels up from Portland. There's talk it'll be going clear to Sacramento in California, maybe next year."

"Jacksonville seems a right nice place," Rebecca said wistfully. "I saw shops. There's many a house like yours—milled lumber."

" 'Tis nice. Since the Territory's expandin' this way our little Jacksonville is growin' and smartin' up real nice."

"Gold mines help," Scotty interjected. "Not all this affluence comes from farming. That's still poor man's work."

"And many of us still fit that shoe," Joshua added ruefully.

"Never you mind." Scotty pointed a finger at him. "It's your choice—now stick with it and be happy."

"I'm not complaining"—Joshua glanced at Rebecca—"least not for myself. I could've joined the miners on the Josephine, but I'd have let the farm go beyond recovery."

"My boy," Scotty's deep voice interrupted again, "it's clear you're cut from better stuff than the hard rock ones. You're edging straight toward politics, plain as the nose on your face."

"You've just been listenin' to Jesse Applegate again."

He nodded and settled back with a pleased grin. "Talkin' and plannin'. Jess and me know the size of our influence. We lack the gumption to stick with what it takes to be political. You don't. Men are starting to talk and listen. I hear your name. Especially last August." His heavy brows furrowed and his eyes flashed.

"If you'd been there, we might have decided to send you to Congress instead of that soft-centered Joe Lane."

Joshua threw his head back and laughed. Wiping his eyes, still shaking his head, he said, "That's a joke! Me against Lane? Want me to look like a whipped puppy? Besides, I couldn't sit around forever. You and I both know every political faction in the Territory has been on again, off again. First they wanted to call a convention, but when not enough on their side would rally, it was off again. It's been goin' on like that for years."

Scotty was nodding his agreement and Joshua continued, "You can't get together a state government that people will accept when you can't get the people together to begin with, and then they won't agree on what's important. There's too much fightin' and pulling different directions."

"But that's all settled and done." Scotty thumped his chair to the floor. "Man, it's settled. Now just go be our senator."

Joshua was shaking his head. "Maybe later."

"Don't think you have enough influence? You could have gone in there and pushed railroads. That'll swing plenty of votes."

"We need one, that's certain. The farmers will never make it without. The whole Willamette Valley is a paradise for growing things, but with no market within reach, why plant? Seems the market in California is drying up—they're decidin' down there that plantin's more sure than diggin' gold. We're going to have to range farther afield to peddle our crops."

While Scotty was nodding his agreement, Matilda stirred restlessly. She whispered to Rebecca, "There's a woolen mill in Salem. A machine does it all except what the sheep does."

Scotty turned to his wife. " 'Tain't so. There's a little strippin' of the sheep that takes place before the machinery takes over."

Matilda ignored him. "Later I'll show you some of the goods. Beautiful." She slanted her eyes toward her husband. "Better'n Scotland and Ireland put together."

He looked at her and chuckled. "Scotland and Ireland put together explodes. And quit your teasin'; we'll have our politics, or you ladies will never have your railroads."

In the morning it was raining. For three days they lingered on at Jacksonville while Scotty and Joshua argued politics.

During the three days, Solali and Rebecca learned their way around the MacLennan kitchen, while Eagle roamed the countryside and the men moved between barn and kitchen talking, oblivious to the world around them.

As Solali kneaded bread and stirred the simmering pot of stewed apples, she admitted, "I'd forgotten the pleasure of living like this." Rebecca, tongue-tied with the picture of their past, caught Matilda's curious glance. But Solali's feeble explanation erased the picture of the Indian village from Rebecca's thoughts. She had simply said, "We've been cookin' beside the trail over a poor sagebrush fire for too many days."

Now Rebecca added, "It's the food. You know, Matilda, I'd been eating Solali's lumpy mush for—" she gulped and added, "for a long time before—before I found out the lumps were *roasted grasshoppers!*"

There was Matilda's amused glance at Solali, sharing that intimacy which gently scorned white ways. "You did survive, didn't you?" And when Rebecca wrinkled her nose even Solali laughed with Matilda.

After dinner on that final day, Rebecca was able to ask Scotty some of the questions which had been nagging at her. "What else happened at the convention that Joshua missed last August?"

"Well, young lady, how much do you know about making a state?"

"Little."

"It goes this way. First you gotta be a territory. See, when you get a bunch of people livin' together in a spot 'o land, there gets to be problems. Sooner or later there's the question of whose army ya yell for when the goin' gets rough. Rough it was, with the Indians. Seems like you have to do something pretty concrete to get to belong. Like this bunch settin' up constitution."

"And—" Rebecca was becoming impatient with Scotty's teasing.

"Scotty, you'd better be careful with your joshin'; she's been a schoolteacher."

"Oh, beggin' your pardon, lady. All this time I figured you were leadin' me along just to make a good impression. In that case, I'll not only inform you, I'll appoint you his campaign manager—all you have to do is put enough gumption into him to make him see his value and be willin' to put a little knuckle behind his beliefs."

"Fight? Mercy, I don't want Joshua to do that!"

He turned to Joshua. "I'm seein' you have a big job to do. You take her home and educate her all about politics."

"What about the Constitution?" Rebecca asked.

With a chuckle, Scotty settled back in his chair. Joshua's eyes were seeking hers, and then he answered, "Do you remember I told you about this in a letter? Oregon became a territory in '49." As Rebecca looked at him, meeting his eyes, the letters from out of the past became a link, binding them together in a kinship she had nearly forgotten. As Scotty took up the lesson, his voice rumbled in the background as she let the tender memory of those letters circle through her thoughts.

"Applegate." Scotty's voice rose as if to capture her thoughts. "Old man Applegate was in on this from the beginning. He helped write the Territorial Constitution. But Joe Lane was appointed the first Territorial governor."

"And you think Joshua could beat Lane for the senate seat?" Rebecca's voice reflected the awe she was feeling as she looked from one man to the other.

"Scotty's dreamin'," Joshua muttered.

Ignoring him, Scotty said, "You know, there's nothing that makes a man appreciate his country more'n to be out from under it, all by his lonesome. A body likes to feel secure." He

pointed his finger at Rebecca. "I know you're going to say constitution again. That came later. When it did, it gave every
man 320 acres. They voted to exclude slavery from the Territory, but they wouldn't allow any free Negroes." His piercing
gaze centered on Rebecca. "You see, young lady, there's no place
on God's earth that's perfect. If you're going to live in Oregon,
you'll have to be a scrapper like the rest of us."

Rebecca stared up at him. Her thoughts tumbled with emotion. He was inviting her to fight, to have an opinion. In the
past, how badly she had wanted to raise her voice in protest,
how she had suffered with the agony of holding her tongue. She
looked at Joshua smiling at her. A new feeling rose in her, hope
taking wings.

CHAPTER 6

" 'Tis all downhill, all the way home," Joshua had announced when they reached the summit of the final mountain pass.

Since leaving the MacLennan's in Jacksonville, even the horses found it impossible to move quickly. This was home and they all knew it. Now they meandered the woods and valleys slowly, savoring the belonging. As they rode down the length of the Willamette, marveling at its crashing descent, the river gorge widened and gentled, and the valley spread before them.

The rolling meadows and rounded hills with their crowns of fir and hemlock seemed groomed, disciplined into civilization. It was nearly impossible to believe that the distant field had always been meadow green, that the clump of wild plum was there by happenstance, not design. That curve of hill and wind-break of pine seemed deliberately cultivated to surround the distant log cabin.

As they wandered down the valley, curious eyes and friendly faces met them at every door, demanding that they stop. While Rebecca probed the ways of life in the valley and studied the cabins and their occupants, Joshua and the men talked. Bending over split-rail fences, they analyzed the August convention and the new Constitution. "Politics, politics," her hostesses would say, smiling.

More likely than not, Rebecca was discovering, Joshua was well known by all the people they greeted.

As Rebecca shared tea and chatter, she recognized the authority and influence that seemed to come through all Joshua's conversations. The faces tilted upward, hanging on his words.

Later as they rode, he brooded, "Up the valley there's bad feelings. Seems people are sidin' up with the South and muttering about needin' slaves if we're to progress. That's the hook they used in the South." He turned to look at her. "See, in the beginning the southerners were in favor of abolition. Then came the surge in cotton production. The growing market made them change their minds. Said they'd never make it without slaves."

"They could have hired," Rebecca objected.

"That cuts the profits," Joshua said, adding, " 'Tis hard to be charitable when there's such an easy way to get rich."

The next day they rode off the trail to stop at a farmhouse. "I know it's a delay," Joshua said, "but these are people I want you to meet."

At first approach, the cabin looked like all the others they had passed. But as the horses reached the fence, Rebecca changed her mind. *There's a certain neatness,* she thought; *seems like these folks are really proud of their place.* She was still noticing that not a weed or stick of wood marred the scene of order when Joshua cupped his hands around his mouth and shouted. People poured from the tiny cabin.

Rebecca hadn't time for astonishment, even when she saw the people were Indian. She had been in their presence only a few minutes when she realized they were Christians.

When they finally moved on again, Joshua told her about them, and his respect for them was evident in his words. "You saw them. Their life is a testimony just like that Indian Palmer met. God changes men for the good, no matter what their past has been. Every red man in the Territory must be given a chance like these people." The passion of his feelings came through and Solali turned to look at Joshua. Her eyes were still wide with wonder at all she had seen. Now a smile touched her lips, but she rode on without speaking.

When they finally turned east into the valley Joshua called home, Rebecca found herself hanging back, suddenly timid. Joshua pulled his horse in close to her and studied her face. "We're leavin' the Willamette River," he turned to point. "See, she's continuing on north while we're headed east up the McKenzie. That's our river," he explained again. "Pa and I have land just the other side of it."

Rebecca was trying to listen, but her thoughts were full of Joshua's mother, Cynthia, and that old feeling. From out of the past the words welled up in her memory: *Cynthia doesn't want me.* Her eyes sought Joshua's. But she remembered, too, those things he had said just before they arrived at Jacksonville. He didn't want her beholden; maybe he didn't want her either.

Now she saw his eyes wary, full of the unsaid things. "Becky"—he bent close and his eyes begged her to understand—"you've made me promise silence, and I'm fearful. Pa and Ma are bad enough, but the others—they'll deal with you harshly. I know my neighbors. There's a kinship around these parts that makes secrets hard to keep. They think they've got to know everything about a body."

He dropped his hand; she was still shaking her head.

"Don't worry." There was just a touch of impatience in his voice. "I'll not be the one to say it. I hear you, and I promise I'll not say a thing to them. But you'll have to live with it."

Rebecca straightened and stared at him. A retort burned on her lips, but suddenly she was caught. The idea was liberation, freedom. He was guessing, and a smile touched his lips as his words echoed her thoughts. "From this day on, the past is gone. Bury it, just like it never existed." He took a deep breath: "Becky, for me that's how it is. I hold you that way—please."

Quietly she folded her hands across the saddle and the tears rolled down her cheeks. "Buried, done," she whispered. She guided her horse down the hill after him as he moved to catch up with Solali and Eagle.

At the very end of the little caravan, even behind the pack animals led by Eagle, Rebecca rode into her new life, conscious of new thoughts. Joshua's words, including all the unsaid ones, made Rebecca realize just what this journey was meaning. "It's past, gone," she whispered to herself as she took a deep breath. But she couldn't forget she was still ignoring that small dead spot in her heart.

At the bottom of the hill the road flattened out. Now they

rode into a narrow valley, bowled between rolling hills wooded with hemlock and fir. They passed plowed fields and pastures filled with cattle. Houses and barns marked the farms. Now there was a line of fence and the military parade of young fruit trees.

The McKenzie River caught up with them and twisted past one farm after another as it plunged downward to meet the Willamette. Crashing over lips of tumbled stone fringed with fern, the river took on character. Rebecca felt its force, its energy as it plunged down the mountainside in front of them.

As they traveled, the day which had begun damp and cool began to mellow and warm. The sun was wringing sweetly-scented mists from the earth. With each step that Rebecca's horse took, she felt a new thrust to life. There was an underlying excitement, a stir toward delight; but her troubled senses scarcely dared trust the urge.

The sun was setting when their road narrowed and the McKenzie quieted. Joshua dropped back to ride with her. "We'll be there soon," he reported. "In a bit we'll be passing through Waltstown. There's a general store, a blacksmith shop, a school, and a church. Not much else, but it's a start."

"What kind of a church?" she asked curiously.

"Kind?" he echoed, looking surprised. "I don't reckon it has a tag. Seems around here people aren't too fussy." He frowned. " 'Tis not like what you've known in the past."

As he urged his horse forward, Rebecca thoughtfully studied his back, wondering how Joshua really felt about her past. There was that stigma. Even in Utah Territory it was well known how those outside the Territory regarded plural wives. Rebecca sighed, and the ever-present burden on her heart claimed her attention.

Blue shadows were piling up under the fir and hemlock when, with a shout, Joshua cut in front of the pack animals and headed down the twin ruts winding through meadow grass. "This way!" his call drifted back to them.

Briefly Rebecca reined her mount and watched Eagle cut through the grass to join Joshua. They had left the road mounting the slope to the foothills; their path, moving at right angles to the road, was heading along the valley through meadows lush and green. Between their trail and the mountains the McKenzie River churned toward them.

Rebecca allowed her horse to follow the group, and Solali hung back to ride with her. "This is my home," she stated flatly. Rebecca glanced at her, wondering if she were disappointed that the journey was nearly ended. Solali was looking around now with interest, and Rebecca dismissed the thought with a shrug.

It was a peaceful ride through tall bushes clumped close to the water and the scattering of evergreens that lined the road. Just ahead a stream of smoke announced a cabin. But Joshua didn't slow. He gave a quick wave of his hat to the distant figure by the barn and hurried on. Now they plunged down a grassy slope and at the far reach of the valley, snugged near the up-slope of the mountains, was another cabin. There were the soft greens and white of young fruit trees nearby. Behind them there were corrals and a barn. A line of fence drew her eyes to the brilliance of green-gold. "That's grain," Solali remarked, and then added, "This must be Joshua's farm" This time her voice had a happy lilt. Rebecca turned her attention to the house.

As they walked their horses slowly toward it, she could see that it was much larger than the homes they had been seeing down Waltstown way. It was built of logs. The late afternoon sun flooded the house with light, warming the varied brown of the logs and giving a sparkle to the windows that flanked the door. While they continued to ride toward it, Rebecca sensed the natural fitness of the gentle brown structure with the rolling hills around it. It was in harmony with the land. From spreading veranda to the massive chimney of river stones, she felt the peace of it. And she was knowing how well it fit the man who was riding toward it.

Rebecca pulled on the reins. There was a spot of color on the veranda. That would be Cynthia. As the woman moved down the path, Rebecca's hand stole to her throat. The cord biting into her neck reminded her. Quickly she snatched the black furry hood from her shoulders and stuffed it under the rabbit-skin robe. Her trembling fingers rubbed at the grimy buckskin and tugged at the worn fringe.

"Oh dear, I look so terrible," Rebecca mourned. Solali grinned at her and Rebecca reached for her. "Solali, I'm so glad that you've come with us. I don't think I could face this alone." She hesitated a moment and then spoke quickly, fearful of how Solali would take it all. "Solali, I've asked Joshua to say nothing about our past. You know and I know—" Her voice trailed away. Solali's eyes widened as she looked at Rebecca, but before there was time for an answer, Cynthia was beside Rebecca.

The woman's hair was gray now and her face was lined. Held in the clasp of her arms, Rebecca discovered that her body was soft and warm. For a moment there was that old yearning for mother love, and then she was realizing how long it had been since those long ago days beside the Mississippi.

But when Cynthia held her off to study her face, Rebecca was even more deeply conscious of the passage of time. There were more hugs and pats and warm welcoming words. But in Rebecca's mind lingered Cynthia's shocked expression and the way that expression had included dark questions. But her arm around Rebecca as they walked toward the house was warm and firm. Cynthia was doing the talking, placing Rebecca back into the circle of their lives. "Pa's up the way, a'workin' at buildin' us our own little house. Matt's married and livin' down close to Salem. His Amy is a right pretty girl, delicate like a little posy." She added, "They're expecting their first young'un soon. Jamie's been hirin' out down at the wharfs at Champoeg. There's a lot of shipping goin' on down there." Now she sighed and said, "Course, Prue's still back in Illinois. Just think, if they'd come, then we'd all be here together, just like old times." Rebecca was thinking that her voice didn't carry the message her words did, but she dismissed the thought as Cynthia went back to her conversation. "All along the way here, they're raisin' grain. Then they're a'shippin' it down the Willamette to the Columbia, then out to the ocean."

Her voice was filled with awe, "Land, it seems strange to be thinkin' of the foreigners eating bread made outta our grain. Even the Russians are buying it." Now she focused on Rebecca again. "He's making a good living down there and he's sparking a girl, my Jamie is. She's part Indian." She sighed, "Women are scarce around here. But," she added quickly, "there's no call to fuss about her being Indian." She slanted a glance toward Solali.

"Jamie," Rebecca marveled, "little Jamie grown and courtin'!" They had moved across the veranda and through the open door and Rebecca stopped to look around. The room they entered was large and bright with light from the big windows on each side of the door. A stone fireplace filled the end wall. To her left an open door revealed a bedroom. Cozied between the end of the fireplace and another door on the right was a stairway angling upward.

On the right Rebecca could see the big kitchen. A shiny black stove dominated the center of the room.

"See," Joshua was explaining as he waved toward the kitchen, "in the beginning, the kitchen was my cabin and the rest of the house just grew from it."

"Joshua and his pa hauled all those river stones up and dumped them outside the door to the cabin." Cynthia pointed to the fireplace. "I declare, they didn't want to move them again, so they just built the fireplace where they dropped them."

Joshua laughed and picked up Rebecca's trunk. Cynthia looked at it and then cocked her head at Rebecca. "So, it did finally catch up with you," she remarked slowly. Again she looked at Rebecca with those questions in her eyes. "I didn't have much faith in that stage when I sent it off."

Rebecca caught her breath and bit her tongue to keep from spilling a torrent of questions about the trunk. How badly she wanted to know just when it had reached Great Salt Lake City. With a sigh she turned to follow Joshua up the stairs. As she climbed the stairs, she muttered to herself, "I guess turnabout's fair." If Cynthia's questions must remain unasked, then Rebecca dare not admit her own.

Beyond the shining windowpanes of the cozy room she and Solali were to share, Rebecca could see the barn and corral. An apple tree outside the window was making promises with its show of blossoms. As memories of her favorite apple tree back in Illinois flooded over her, Rebecca realized with a start, her birthday had just passed.

Joshua said, "Shall I place the trunk under the window so you can lean on it and smell the apple blossoms?" She was both pleased and dismayed that he would remember the thirteen-year-old girl of so long ago leaning on her window sill and peering through the apple-tree branches at him.

"Joshua"—there was a painful pressure around her heart from the old memories—"life doesn't go back. Some things just can't happen again."

"Yes, they do, Becka. If there's hope enough, they can happen again." Abruptly he leaned across the trunk and pushed the window open.

"Joshua," Rebecca warned, "you'll fall out."

"No, I won't." He plucked a branch and backed into the room. "There. Until apple time, this must do." He held out the branch of delicate blooms and slowly Rebecca reached for it. She tried desperately to hide her tears in the blossoms as she hunted for words.

"Just tell me that you won't go running off to Oregon this time," she finally managed.

"I cross my heart," he said. "No more running. We've both had enough to last a lifetime. Besides, we're here! This is Oregon, and now life begins. It's all new." His eyes were reminding her there was no past.

She ducked her head and he touched her chin. "No more tears, ever," he said gently, "but may I have just one smile?"

She turned away and sniffed appealingly. "I'd be obliged if you'd just let me owe it to you."

Joshua walked slowly down the stairs. His mother was waiting below. She stood hesitant, awkward and he reached out to give her a quick hug. "Don't look like that. Everything will be just fine. Give her time. Just, please, don't question her. The past is mighty painful." His eyes were demanding and for a moment she couldn't move beyond them.

"She's so—" her voice faltered.

"Old?" He brought the blunt word out. "Mother, Rebecca is twenty-seven years old. You haven't seen her for eleven years.

I haven't seen her since she was a scrawny little girl of thirteen, all big blue eyes and mounds of taffy hair. We all change, even you." He bent over to pinch her rosy cheek. More gently now he said, "Me thinks it would be best to forget about tying links to the past and be content with helping her build a new life."

"You're talking brave, like saying so makes the years already gone by as if they never were."

He was lifting his stubborn chin toward his mother in a way he hadn't done since he was a lad. He delivered the flat statement, "They weren't."

Her eyes met his again and he saw the decision being made. For now the dark questions were being pushed aside. She blinked and patted his arm.

"Thanks, Ma."

CHAPTER 7

Rebecca, leaning over the kitchen table, moved her lips silently as she read the newspaper spread before her. It was almost more than she could grasp. She mouthed the words again. The back door opened and Joshua came into the kitchen carrying a basket filled with greens, peas, and early beets.

"Joshua," Rebecca said as she marked the spot, "will you come here, please? I can't believe the terrible things this paper says. Is this man foolin'? Why, that's terrible language to be using about somebody!"

"You're reading the *Statesman*," Joshua replied. "Editor Bush is a mighty powerful voice in the Territory."

"I don't like the way he's speaking," Rebecca muttered, turning back to the paper.

" 'Tis frontier talk. There's no sweetness and light about the Oregonians. No man with a gentle voice is likely to be heard about here," Joshua continued as he dumped his load into the washtub. "Good politics involves a little swingin' of the fists."

"But talk like that? Sounds like he's not too fond of the delegate to Congress. Isn't that General Joseph Lane, and isn't he the man you said was governor at one time?"

"Yes to both."

"Why's Bush sliding around and giving him a fictitious name if everybody's guessing it's Lane anyway?"

He shrugged. "That's part of the game. Seems to add to the excitement if you're having to dig through the garbage and the funny names to figure out who it'd be. Seems a body stands a better chance of getting a man's attention if the words aren't plain old grammar-school words." Rebecca turned back to the newspaper.

After a moment Joshua said, "The *Statesman* was the voice of Oregon for a long time. Don't know how much longer Bush'll be able to hang on to the hat. It's about broke him. Had the job of printing the Territorial laws. They wanted 500 copies. Also had the job of printin' up the Territorial legislature session laws back in '54 or '55. All that printed material plus his new press was lost at sea when the ship carrying it sank.

"He never did recover his money or his good humor after that. Lane's still trying to get hold of some money back in Washington to pay for the printing of the laws of the Territory. He's also trying to get Congress to foot the bill for the Indian wars."

Joshua took time to lift a dipper of water to his lips. "Ah, that's good. It's getting hot out there." He continued, "About the money for the Indian wars: General Wool wasn't too impressed with the claims Washington and Oregon Territories set forth, and the money is mighty slow comin'. Could explain why everybody's taking it out on Lane. Now there's rumblin' among his own party. They're saying that Lane's responsible for delaying the statehood bill."

"Why ever would he do that?"

"He isn't. Out here, Oregon way, it's kinda hard to believe that the most important work on the docket in Washington isn't gettin' the bid for Oregon's statehood approved."

"You sound as if you know what's going on back there."

Joshua shrugged. "Any man with a reasonable head on his shoulders agrees that Lane's doing right."

"If that's so, why's Scotty unhappy with the man?"

"You got to understand—Scotty's radically opposed to slavery. Doesn't sound like much to say that. Seems at least half the Territory's that way, but Jacksonville and most of the southern part of the Territory is in favor of slavery."

"But they wrote 'no slavery' in the Constitution, didn't they? Doesn't that mean the matter's settled?"

Joshua straightened and turned to Rebecca. Slowly he said, "This nation is being torn apart over the slavery issue. Sooner or later men are going to take sides and it will be more than fists a'flying before it's all over."

Rebecca looked down at the paper. The cruel words seemed to leap out at her. The insinuations and veiled threats became more than childish indignities. Slowly her hand crept to her throat.

"Rebecca, don't—take it like that," Joshua begged. He was standing close to her, looking down. The bright light of the midday sun touched his face and she looked into his troubled eyes. She took her hand from her throat, hesitated a moment and then, taking a step nearer, she dropped her hand across his shoulder and peered at him.

"Why, Joshua," she said with surprise. "I've just now realized it. Your eyes have flecks of green in them. *That's* why I think of sunlit forests when I think of you!"

His eyes were changing, darkening. Ducking his head, he pressed his bearded face against the hand resting lightly on his shoulder. "Remember," his voice was muffled, "Scotty said I was to be educating you. You best be quiet and listen."

The moment that should have been captured in lighthearted laughter stretched and flattened. A fly buzzed against the window. Slowly Rebecca moved, her hand dropped and she sighed.

Turning from the table, she said, "Seems at times I still have a difficulty fastening my thoughts on a subject and keeping them there." She looked apologetically at him, wanting desperately to pour out her feelings, begging him to have patience for just a little longer.

Matter-of-factly he turned back to his task. As he poured cold water into the tub he said, "The corn's not much good around here. I knew it wouldn't be; there's just not enough of the good hot weather here, but I can't help hankerin' for the roasting ears we grew back home. There's a spot up the side of the hill, surrounded by rocks and facing south. Come next year. I'll try my luck plantin' up there."

In less than a week it would be June. Almost six weeks had passed since Rebecca had arrived in Oregon. Today as she stood in the doorway of Joshua's house looking down the valley toward Waltstown, she mused over the changes that she had seen taking place.

It seemed she and Solali were being accepted into the community with little fuss. She was feeling the acceptance and even now beginning to relax into it. If there were undercurrents of question, she was unaware of it.

Without having willed it, she knew life was picking a new pattern, and she was knowing how she must live in order to keep settled forever the dust of her past.

Because she had determined she would not acknowledge that past, she found she must demand of herself a new discipline. There must be no fragment of living or thought to point to the life behind. She must ignore the weak arm and force it to behave like its companion. Without a hesitation in her step, she must move as if her serene woman-life had never been interrupted.

But there were those moments when the past would tumble into her thoughts, even though she was learning how to catch herself quickly. She knew that when the dark pictures and heavy moods threatened her, they could sweep from her mind everything, even the knowledge of the next ingredient for the bread she was mixing.

If there was primary satisfaction in these beginning days in Oregon, she found it in thinking that Cynthia never guessed her deepest feelings or sensed the despair life had heaped upon her.

Joshua's household had also accepted Solali as easily as a stone slipping into a quiet pool. If Cynthia questioned the presence of a woman whom she and her neighbors had considered savage, her placid face never revealed it. But then, it was easy to overlook Solali. Her hands were busy at the right time and her quiet efficiency kept her beyond even Cynthia's reproach.

Eagle was another problem.

From his dress to his stoic silence, Eagle was decidedly Indian. The braids and the buckskin didn't give way to overalls and boots, even when Solali assumed the dress of the white woman. Fortunately for all concerned, Eagle's restless energy wouldn't harbor the stricture of house and farm. When Rebecca saw Cynthia's reaction to the man, she was relieved to see him go, knowing it would be easier for Cynthia to accept the gentle Solali when Eagle wasn't around to remind them of the differences. And increasingly, Rebecca needed Solali's quiet presence there.

Now Rebecca was thinking about the scene late one afternoon last week. It still made her uneasy. Rebecca had been sitting alone and quiet beside the cold fireplace when Cynthia walked into the house carrying a bolt of dark blue calico sprigged with pink roses.

As Rebecca stood up, Cynthia held the cloth up to her. "Right pretty, being you're a towhead. You're gettin' pink in your cheeks again and the roses will help."

"That's nice." They turned. Joshua stood in the doorway watching, with an admiring, questioning look.

Solali came in behind him, and her wistfulness was revealed in her face and fingers as she bent to touch the cloth. "Oh, it's beautiful!"

Cynthia frowned when Solali spoke, questioning, Rebecca knew, how an Indian woman could speak English as easily as a white woman.

Cynthia's only comment was, "Rebecca needs a new dress. I spotted this at the store last week and knew 'twas made for her."

"It takes me back in time," Rebecca whispered with a catch in her voice. "You telling me to hold still, then shaking your head because I'm getting tall."

"Now you're such a little thing."

"But she *is* getting pink in her cheeks." Joshua took the milk pails from Solali and left the house. After lingering a moment, Solali followed him. The touch of sadness on the woman's face etched the scene on Rebecca's mind.

One of the biggest adjustments for Rebecca was the Sunday worship services. True, the women wore calico, just as they had back there. True, they carried their dinners to church and shared them under the trees; but there the similarities ended.

From the hymns to the prayer: *Dear Heavenly Father—in*

Jesus' name; from the sermon out of the Book marked Holy Bible, it was different. No longer was she hearing the Prophet's words expounded. Rebecca's mind drank in the truth like a thirsty stallion.

She was hearing the words she had read in secret and learned to love. The promises which had fearfully trembled on her own lips now tumbled in thundering affirmation from the lips of Parson Williams. It was life underlined and emphasized; meanwhile Rebecca must sit primly, not giving way to the wide-eyed wonder she felt.

On these Sabbaths, serenely, quietly, as if it had always been this pattern in the past, she donned Cynthia's extra dress and followed her to church. But never must she allow herself to forget that she was working out a new pattern of living. Sometimes it would all seem easy and natural; at other times she would catch that shadowed look in Joshua's eyes or see Solali's questioning glance.

Sometimes community acceptance could be easy as Katy Horton's sliding down the pew and offering the hymnal. But sometimes, particularly after church when the congregation met under the trees for dinner, she had to work hard to fit herself into the new way of life. Now she found herself timidly reaching out, daring to express her thoughts and feelings.

Sometimes, while the women spread their fried chicken and apple pies across the tables set up under the trees, the men would cluster around a new horse and hotly discuss the latest news from Washington. When their voices rose and the gossip about Lane or his buddy, Asahel Bush, turned to politics, Rebecca would find herself inching toward them.

Scotty MacLennan had whetted her political appetite and challenged her mind. Now as the high tide of emotion erupted from the men, she found herself strangely drawn. Sometimes she dared ask a question. "At the Constitutional Convention, was there more'n just the Democrats there?"

Impatiently—after all, she was a woman—"Yes, only about two-thirds of them were Democrats. There was a Republican there. Don't know his name. There were two Whigs and a handful of independents. 'Twas a bunch of different ones too, includin' some Free Soilers."

Others added their voice. "I'd like to see Dryer—he's the editor of *The Oregonian*—head for the Republican side."

"Aw, he's got his head in the sand. He'll never admit the Whigs are done, washed up. It was the slavery issue that done 'em in way back in '53."

"Jesse Applegate was there. Still hanging in there as an independent. Shrewd, huh? Waiting to see which way the ball bounces. . . ." And they were off again, forgetting her.

Joshua was standing beside her now, and Rebecca whispered, "More'n one party and no one telling them how to vote. Think of that!" Joshua threw her a sharp glance and the concern she saw reminded her of their secret. This was Oregon. She turned back to the tables.

As she helped lift the baskets and spread the tablecloth, she was fussing at herself. What a slippery thing the tongue was! How easy it was to trip up herself. Joshua had been more careful than she. One more word and surely these people would know. They would recognize that the only place hereabouts where there was only one party and one voice would be Utah Territory. Or did they even know?

Over fried apple pies, the arguments erupted again. "I'll tell you why Asahel Bush's Clique is losing out. It's his fault as much as anyone. He's been tryin' to run the Democratic party since '55. He don't care what the doctrine of the party is; he's just for it. You'd think a body who isn't a Democrat is ignorant. He's sayin' right now that there ain't to be a public office for that other bunch, the Nothings. I tell you, one of these days he'll get his up-and-comin's. And I hope the Republicans give it to 'im."

"You Republican?"

"Naw, I'm a good Democrat, but—"

"Well, the Republicans'll never make it if they don't get a bunch to rally 'round the flag pretty soon."

"Had a good start in the November '56 Convention. A Republican was elected enrolling clerk."

"Some think that's no honor." And with that flat statement,

the group broke apart. A few returned to the table for another fried pie while a game of horseshoes ended the politics and the women sighed at the mess left behind.

The days of nearly constant rain gave way to sun and warmth. The garden brimmed with produce and on the hillside behind the house the wild berries were ripening.

The sight of the wild blackberries sent Rebecca into the house that June afternoon searching out Solali to help her pick the fruit. As Rebecca walked through the house and up the stairs, she sensed the quietness, feeling it fasten its claim upon her. She also felt a waiting in the quietness—but for what? She sighed.

The door of the room she shared with Solali was closed. Without thought, she turned the knob and entered. Solali was on her knees before the trunk, holding Rebecca's Bible. In the seconds before the woman moved, Rebecca saw first the Book and then the dress that Solali wore. The dark blue calico with the pink roses fit Solali as if it had been made for her.

"I do believe you look better in it!" Rebecca said, recovering quickly.

Slowly Solali stood to her feet. She closed the Bible and placed it on the bed. When she turned the mixture of emotion on her face touched Rebecca. "Oh, Solali, don't be embarrassed. I don't mind that you wear the dress."

"But *she* would."

"Yes," Rebecca said thoughtfully, sensing the undercurrents that Solali had noticed in the household. "But Cynthia is that way. Do you know that I am an outsider, too? Always, even back when she took me into their home as a little girl. She was kind to me, always, but I never forgot that I was the outsider."

"It is different with me." She looked down at the dress and carefully spread its folds. "It is beautifully made, but when I put it on I feel the lack in me. The Indian dress fits me. Then I feel at home."

"At one time you dressed like this. You were raised to calico, not the Indian dress."

She was nodding. "This has been good, this time here. I

wanted to see if I could wear the dress, be the white woman again."

"You're wanting to live like this."

While her fingers fumbled with the buttons on the dress, she nodded. "I don't know how to explain it. Rebecca, until you came to the village of my people, I was content. Joyfully I had slipped back into their ways." Fingering the buttons she sighed, "I had nearly forgotten the past, the log cabin and Mormon quilts, the milk and eggs and fresh bread. In smelling the woodsmoke and tanning skins and drying meat—in mixing and baking our bread made from rice grass seeds and the pollen of cattails for the little ones, I was forgetting."

She turned to gesture toward the Book. "Can you understand? I turned my back on the teachings of the Mormons and tried to pick up again the ways of my people. I would have been content to forget the reading of white man's books if you hadn't brought this one. The first ten summers I had lived with my people had grown dim. The next eight summers with the Mormons I knew I must push from my thoughts. But now." She stopped and pulled off the dress and reached for her own frock. Smoothing her hair and fastening the buttons she said. "I kept thinking the clothes and the Book could change me."

"Why do you want to change?" Rebecca frowned as she asked the question.

"I'm not certain why. When you first came to the village you talked about the Book."

"When I was sick?" Rebecca asked in a low voice.

"Yes, in the worst of the time you begged for it. It was almost as if it was a charm you believed in, that you must touch it."

"Not magic, Solali," Rebecca said. She was trying desperately to forget about the time of her illness and to bring back all those thoughts and remember the words. How could she explain the ideas that made the Book so important?

"When Eagle first brought the Book to the village, you clung to it as if you were afraid to let it out of your sight. Since we've come here, you seem to—well, isn't it important anymore? Is it because Joshua is with you now? Why have you changed?"

Rebecca couldn't answer. She was busy with her own painful

thoughts. Now Solali said, "I'm nagged by the Book. I want to discover what is important about it all. And, then, I want to become a part of all this new way to live."

"But you won't even go to church with us on the Sabbath."

Solali looked bewildered, "But that's what the Mormons do. Is there really a difference?"

Shocked, Rebecca stared at Solali. In her mind the differences began lining up. But even as she contemplated them, Solali's bewildered expression informed her of her failure.

Rebecca dropped her head, whispering, "Solali, I'm sorry. I've taken and taken of your kindness and I haven't given you a thing. In spite of how it has seemed, this really is the most important part of my life." She touched the Book, continuing, "Please forgive me, and right now I'll change it all." She stepped toward Solali and hugged her. "Come help me pick berries, and I'll tell you about Jesus."

The berries plunked slowly into the pails. But that was all right; Rebecca was explaining some very important truths, and she needed both arms to gesture, threatening the loaded bushes and half-empty pail. Words were so limiting. She had explained about sin and the righteous God. She tried to detail the story of the covenants and give life and passion to the picture of God, and then create a clear picture of a loving Savior in Jesus Christ. She quoted John 3:16 and the Romans passages telling of man's sin.

"There's just no hope without Jesus. God said it in the Old Testament, and the Apostles repeated it in the New. Jesus said He was the way and the truth and life." In frustration her tired arms dropped.

And Solali spoke around her puzzled frown. "You are thinking to persuade me? You are so passionate to convince me that you are right. Rebecca, if the Book is true, if it shows the right way, why can't I read it myself and discover what I must believe?"

Slowly Rebecca sat down on a rock. "You mean I don't have to convince you that you must throw out Mormonism and accept this?"

"I have already thrown out Mormonism. It did nothing for

the dark inside of me, the fear. You see, you forget that no matter the color of the skin, down underneath, we are the same. I don't have to be persuaded to be fearful of God. It is there. Rebecca, I didn't leave the Mormon way because they were mean to me. I left because I must find peace, and it wasn't in the Mormon faith. Now you say it is all in this Book. Let me read it. I take it slowly, with much thought, anything that is given to me. Will your God be patient with me while I learn to listen to Him?"

"Yes, Solali," Rebecca whispered, humbled, torn by her wild emotions and Solali's quiet, rational statement. "Yes, and I guess I can quit yelling that He loves you."

Her eyes widened thoughtfully. After a moment she nodded, saying, "But yes. It is all a pathway of love, isn't it? From the beginning until the end. Why, if that is so, and if the way gives such peace, is it so difficult?" Now she turned a stern glance down on Rebecca. "And why do you forget the love?"

"Have I?" she mourned. "Oh, Solali, have I forgotten it?"

"Could it be there's more to His love than you know?" Again Solali's eyes were wide with questions, and there was a beginning excitement in them.

CHAPTER 8

It was July. In the fields beyond the house the winter wheat was a blaze of yellow, moving gently to the touch of wind. Today Solali, Rebecca, and Cynthia sat on the veranda where they could feel the same breeze that moved the wheat. Each held a piece of calico generously patterned with vivid flowers.

As Rebecca's needle reluctantly poked in and out of the fabric she held, she was watching the wheat. While it bent in gentle waves, she was feeling a dreamy contentment wrap her. "Here in this place it is so peaceful and good, it's terribly hard to think of pain and fear and sorrow," hardly realizing she spoke aloud.

She saw Cynthia's eyebrows arch in surprise and Solali glanced quickly at her. Hastily Rebecca said, "I'm thinking of Mrs. Hanson. I heard tell her mentioning the journey into Oregon Territory—the troubles," she babbled on. "It's hard to believe people can come through that and be at peace once again." There was silence while the needles moved rapidly through the cloth.

Cynthia sighed and said, "A time back I said I'd be content forever if I could get me a cookstove. You remember me sayin' that, don't you, Rebecca?" She nodded without taking her eyes off the sewing. Cynthia continued, "Well, now I'm thinking how nice it'd be to have one of those sewing machines. Mrs. Collins has a picture of one. Seems a body could get one shipped around for a wee price. Seems they might even have one or two in San Francisco looking to be sold."

"Now, Cynthia," Rebecca murmured, "why do you want a sewing machine? There's scarcely any calico to be had in the stores in Waltstown. If Mrs. Collins hadn't been willing to part with this piece, Solali would have waited until spring for a dress."

"Things are better in Salem and Portland. When we first came, nothin' was to be had from the States. Seems they were losing ships all too often. It was hard—everything had to come around first off. Before then, they didn't even have flour mills, and the flour was shipped around. Now look, we're shippin' it all over, even as far as Hawaii. Lands a'livin', they talked about wearing animal skins and carving plates out of wood. Things are easy now, compared." Cynthia shifted and sighed.

Rebecca was nodding. "Mrs. Hanson was telling me about those times. She came to the Territory with the Applegate bunch. Her telling me about the trip down the Columbia was enough to scare the wits out of me! No wonder they worked so hard to get in this cutoff up from California way."

" 'Tis better," Cynthia added, "but there's still no wagon road along the Columbia. There's just not enough room along the canyon to make it safe for families to go over. They've taken cattle along the road since first off, but they've lost a sizable bunch, too."

Rebecca was still shaking her head. "Seems it couldn't be worse than the river. Mrs. Hanson says the Applegate family lost two boys when their boat went over. Law, when I think of those wild currents and the falls and all—"

"Leastwise," Cynthia interrupted, "it would have taken you weeks longer to get here. That's why this area didn't start settling right off. The richest land in the whole Territory was the hardest to get to until the Applegates cut through here."

She stood up. "Well, I guess I should take some water to Joshua. I'd expected his pa to be by this afternoon early, but I guess he's so caught up in buildin' that house he can't be bothered."

"It's going to be a pretty place." Solali lifted her face from the sewing. "All that milled lumber makes it fancy. Heard him tell Joshua he'll paint it white just like the places in town."

" 'Nother year and these log places will be out of style,"
Cynthia said comfortably. "That new mill in Eugene is sure
turning out the lumber."

"I love this place." Rebecca glanced up at the mellowed logs
of Joshua's house. "Inside, with the planed walls, it's as neat
as any of the fancy clapboard houses." She got to her feet. "Here,
I'll take water to Joshua. I'm so tired of sitting I'm about to
stab myself with that needle. You like sitting, and Solali has a
heart to finish her dress; let me go." Cynthia nodded and settled
back with a sigh.

Rebecca filled the little tin jug at the well and set off across
the fields toward the distant line of trees and the ring of the
axe. Just beyond them she knew Joshua was cutting wood. The
water sloshed against her skirt and the coldness was a shock
measured by the heat of the day. She walked quickly, glad to
be free of the sewing.

Trudging along the edge of the wheatfield, Rebecca mused
on the changes that were taking place in Solali. It was obvious
that she was responding to the Book and the story of Christ,
but it was puzzling to watch the evidence of struggle going on
in her. At times the Indian woman seemed content, but there
were those unguarded moments when the sadness in her eyes
betrayed other feelings. Rebecca noticed that when Eagle returned from his mysterious forays, Solali seemed more determined than ever to adapt to the white man's way of life.

Rebecca reached the edge of the evergreens and paused to
listen. Again she heard the ring of the axe and she headed up
the hill.

As she reached the clearing, Joshua dropped his axe and
stepped back to watch the towering tree slowly lean. With a
mighty crack, it fell, crashing to the ground with broken
branches flying.

"Bravo!" Rebecca called as she walked across to him. He
turned to wave and she was suddenly shy. He had removed his
shirt. Chest heaving, he wiped his sweating face and waited for
the water she was carrying.

"Just in time," He grinned down at her and reached for the
jug.

"Don't drink too much," she cautioned. "Your face is as red as fire."

"You've bright cheeks too. Come sit in the shade with me." She followed him to the felled log. "It's old; there won't be fresh pitch," he said as she poked at it with an exploring toe.

"It's nice up here—the piney fresh-cut wood smell. I love it." She turned to smile at him and noticed the leather thong about his neck. From it dangled a gold ring. She ducked her head, recalling that snowy night in Utah Territory when he had carried her from the horse to the wayside inn. Through her slipping consciousness she remembered there had been the sharp cut of cold metal against her colder cheek. It must have been the ring.

"You've noticed the ring," he said. "It's from the gold I mined in California." His voice teased lightly, "I must prove I've been there."

"But why don't you wear it?" She could have bitten her tongue. It was obvious.

"It's too small." Still the teasing note, "There was only enough gold to make a ring this big. Wanna try it for size?"

And now there was the echo of a long-ago letter: *"Becky, it's you and me for the green forests of Oregon. I think I'd better snatch you before someone else does."*

She turned away, desperately trying to find a safer subject. "This is a pleasant spot. It's pretty well cleared. You planning on building here?"

"No, not unless you and Solali won't let me stay at the house. It's cleared only for the timber." He hesitated and then added, "You know, Pa's building on his land and the house is about done."

The thought swung between them like the ring on its thong, and there was nothing she could find to say. Rebecca's hand drifted toward her throat. He reached for it. "You needn't do that."

"What?"

"I've noticed that when someone backs you into the corner, you grab for your throat. I'm not pressuring you, Becky. I'm content to wait."

She turned. "I—I've got to be getting back to my sewing." He walked through the trees with her.

"I wish Eagle would put in an appearance right now. I could sure use a little help with the wheat." There was a touch of curiosity in his eyes as he looked down at her.

"I'm sure I don't understand why he comes and goes so mysteriously," she murmured.

"It's Solali. Haven't you guessed?"

"I'd wondered." She turned. "Joshua, I feel her wanting to break with the Indian life. After all, she spent nearly half of her life with white people and it's bound to make a difference in how she feels."

"Yet she left them."

"It was the plural marriage. She hasn't said too much, but I know how she feels."

Joshua's face was thoughtful. "Do you? Sometime I wish you would make me understand how *you* feel."

She caught her breath and studied his open, troubled face. It was too much. Those things were too much for her to share. He would never be able to accept it all. She turned and walked slowly down the hill, deeply conscious of her sore heart.

Would it ever be possible to bare her soul of all the time of hurt and loneliness—especially to him? "Please, God," she whispered, "that mustn't be. 'Tis bad enough to think back through it all. 'Tis impossible to consider talkin' it out." It felt good to be talking to her Father again.

Even as she was whispering the words, there was a busy part of her mind wondering what it would be like—sharing with another human being all the deep parts of her heart. Was it possible someone could help her understand the turmoil going on inside? There were those thoughts connected with God and how He fit into the whole scheme of things. "There's this feeling," she murmured as she walked back along the field of grain. "I'm having the picture of a great big curtain hanging in my life. On one side's me and on the other there's God. 'Tis all right if that's the way it should be, but why am I feeling otherwise?"

There was Solali's question. Was it possible that God's love could penetrate the curtain?

CHAPTER 9

Rebecca, beside the table in the kitchen, was steadying the chair on top of it. Cynthia was standing on the chair, leaning toward the cobwebs with broom in hand. The back door swung open. Rebecca could see it all as it began to happen.

Just as Joshua walked through the door with a basket in his arms, the broom descended crashing to his shoulders.

Rebecca laughed. Standing in the middle of the kitchen full of the smell of rising bread and stewing apples, she laughed. While the midmorning sun slanted through the window and pooled brightness like a flood on that scene, she leaned helplessly against the table, still laughing. Now weak, she felt her hands slipping from her station at the table and tried to signal her powerlessness. Joshua shoved the broom off his shoulders and ran to rescue his mother.

Cynthia sputtered indignantly, "No call to carry on like that." She straightened her apron and allowed Joshua to lift her off the table.

Joshua's face was a study of perplexity. "First time I've been took for an Indian. How's come you didn't go for Pa's gun?"

"Oh, Joshua," Rebecca gasped. "Your face when she hit you with the broom!"

Joshua was chuckling now. " 'Tis many a year since my ma took the broom to me. But I don't recollect getting it in the head before."

With Cynthia's dignity rescued, she too began to smile. " 'Tis silly. It weren't ever that funny. There's cobwebs above the

78

door. I put the chair on the table in order to reach them with the broom. Now if you menfolk had just made this kitchen with nice planed wood like the rest of the house walls, I'd have never been at it like that."

Rebecca was still laughing. "It wasn't you on the table; it was Joshua getting the broom in the face as he walked through the door. And me, not able to think whether to yell or leave the chair."

"Well, we'll do it every day if it'll make you laugh like that." Joshua was smiling down at her.

She caught her breath at the expression in his eyes. "It's everything—" she whispered; "the beautiful day with the sun shining through the window. Even the apples and bread. I—I guess I'm finding it's good to be alive."

"About time, young lady, to be celebrating the Lord's goodness." Joshua's voice was teasing, but the underlying message was there.

He started for the door and paused. Shifting the empty basket, he said, "I've a mind to do like the visiting parson suggested last week." While Rebecca's thoughts fled back to the Sabbath message, he continued. "With Pa gone so much, I'm guessing I'll be the man around here and start family devotions and reading out of the Bible. Every evening."

He disappeared and Cynthia's astonishment kept her silent for a moment before she said, "Well, I declare! I never know what to expect from that young'un." Rebecca was tempted to remind Cynthia that her "young'un" was past thirty years of age.

Cynthia went back to shucking corn, pausing to say, "He's right, this corn's nothing." After a moment she grumbled on, "Since we've been here he's been right sharp about preaching to us about our responsibility to the Lord. Insistent he is about Sabbath worship. It takes a body back. He's not been raised to think goin' to church is important. I'll not take the lip of my own son measuring my life and telling me I'm a'lackin'. Now this is his own land and his own home. We've decided that from the beginning. He was here first, and this place is his choice." She paused and cast a glance toward Rebecca.

"Anyways, it's his place and he's to do as he pleases and we'll all cooperate." Again the sharp glance. While Rebecca was busy wondering why Cynthia would rebel at the Bible reading, she began to understand. Cynthia was expecting Rebecca to rebel, too.

Cynthia dumped the corn into the bucket and continued, "I'll be a mite more content with it all when Pa and I get settled in our own little place. This house is bigger'n a barn. The two of us don't need room like this. That young man looks to be counting on a passel of young'uns."

Rebecca's hand stole to her throat as she fought the memory of that tiny, lonely grave. Cynthia gathered the corn husks and headed for the door. As the door slammed behind her, Rebecca found the bright happy kitchen suddenly a prison, holding thoughts from which she could not escape. She turned and ran toward the stairs.

That evening Joshua kept his promise. At the end of a warm day, past dusk, when the last chore had been done, Joshua carried the lamp to the middle of the kitchen table. "Ma, Becky, Solali," he called.

They settled in their chairs and he opened the Book and began to read. Rebecca watched his strong fingers supporting the Bible, turning the pages. She was lost to the words as she studied him. The lamplight touched his sun-darkened face and brightened his hair. Briefly his eyes caught hers and she concentrated on the words, hearing him read, " 'He restoreth my soul: he leadeth me in the paths of righteousness for his name's sake. Yea, though I walk through the valley of the shadow of death, I will fear no evil: for thou *art* with me; thy rod and thy staff, they comfort me.' " Rebecca felt her lips twist with bitterness and for a moment her mind went dark. Then she heard, " 'Surely goodness and mercy shall follow me all the days of my life: and I will dwell in the house of the Lord for ever.' "

Later, as she started up the stairs behind Solali, Joshua said, "Becky, wait up." The tiny circle of light didn't reach his face, and she was grateful for the shadows that surrounded her.

"I'm sorry that my reading hurt you." The words of denial

rose to Rebecca's lips, but before she could speak, he continued, "I read some more and I couldn't help thinking about you. Please, will you come back to the kitchen for a while and let me read them to you?"

With a sigh of resignation she followed him into the kitchen. They sat down together, and the pale light drew them closer as he opened the Bible. His voice was quiet, meant only for her ears. Again she tried to concentrate on the gentle, deep tones, shutting out the words. But they were compelling and she knew she must listen.

"Rebecca, I don't know how much you believe of all this, but I'm feeling the power in His words. I'm wanting them, like a prayer, for you. Listen and let them in."

"Let them in," she repeated wonderingly.

"Yes. I'm wanting them to become a part of you. They must in order to do their work."

"Joshua, you're talking strange."

"Because I believe there's power in God's Word? He says His word won't come back without doing what it's supposed to do."

The retort was forced from her lips, "Even if I don't want it?"

"But you do. You haven't come this far for nothing. You want all the beauty heaped on you."

It took a long moment for the answer. She was trembling as she said, "Yes, I do."

Tenderly he began, " 'Behold, thou desirest truth in the inward parts: and in the hidden *part* thou shalt make me to know wisdom. Purge me with hyssop, and I shall be clean: wash me, and I shall be whiter than snow. . . . Create in me a clean heart, O God; and renew a right spirit within me. . . . Restore unto me the joy of thy salvation.' "

The words hit Rebecca, twisting through her being, flaming with distorted meaning. She was hearing a long-ago voice. For a moment she pressed her fingers against her forehead, remembering. That woman at the ball in Great Salt Lake City—she had blackened plural marriage with the words given by the Gentiles. "Fallen woman."

Rebecca leaned across the table to face Joshua. "Now tell

me," she whispered the angry words so that her shame would not be spread beyond the room. "Tell me that you must change me until I am worthy of you!"

"Rebecca!" He jumped to his feet and reached for her, but she was gone, flying through the hall and up the stairs.

Rebecca had just begun to dish up the eggs and bacon the next morning when Joshua and his friend Scotty came into the kitchen. "Throw on another plate," Joshua called, "Scott's here."

"I'm back from Salem way," Scotty announced. "And since I didn't find the young, honorable Mr. Smyth down that a'way, I decided to see if he were still livin'." He took the cup of coffee and settled himself at the table.

"The said honorable was busy a'fussin' over his wheat crop," Joshua declared shortly. "Now, tell me what happened."

"Not much. Actually, you'd a'wasted your time goin'. The Republicans had already washed out. They'd nominated candidates, but the whole lot of them threw in the towel. Said the party lacked organization. I've my feelings." He paused to attack the plate in front of him. Later he added, "I've come to the conclusion these fellas were lookin' for an easy win, not a hard fight and a loss. Seems the gumption had gone out of them. 'Course they wouldn't win a seat, but they still needed to get their names in there. You don't become a household name before the next election by hiding out in the barn come this one."

When he returned to the plate of bacon and eggs, Rebecca asked, "And how is Matilda? I enjoyed getting to know her, and I find myself pining for her company."

Scotty began to answer, but Joshua interrupted eagerly, "Tell me what did get accomplished."

"Well, Lane, Smith, and Grover are headed for Washington. I'm hopin' this'll be Lane's last. There's just too much dissatisfaction with the man. Heard tell that he said he doubted a man could be a good Democrat and vote against slavery in Oregon. From a fella who's reluctant to name his side of the fence, that's just too pro-slavery. Trouble is, Lane's just awful political."

"Heard any more about the bill for statehood?" Joshua asked.

"Well, we know it's passed the Senate, but now it's hung up in the House of Representatives. 'Tisn't all Lane's fault. The southern faction in both the Senate and the House are really buckin' the anti-slavery clause."

"I suppose that's causing a lot of rumbles through the whole Territory, but particularly down your way."

"Right you are. The softs have given themselves a new name. They call themselves the National Democratic Party. This whole showdown has them steamin' like a brand-new engine. I expect they'll be spouting off hot air for a long time after we get to be a state."

"Particularly if this thing in Washington comes to a head and splits the country wide open," Joshua added bitterly.

"Now you're not to be saying that," Scotty said soberly. He finished his coffee and held his cup toward Solali. "Gotta admit, Jesse Applegate's about sick over it all. He's been riding the southern part of the Territory and he says the mood's really bad. Some's been tearin' down the flag in parts. Other places there's more fists a'flyin' than words. Didn't expect to see this much restlessness apart from the Indian troubles."

"Does Lane know what's goin' on?"

"Naw. He and Bush aren't even communicatin' now. Bush's gone so soft all he can spout now's Stephen A. Douglas and Popular Sovereignty."

"Well, Lane asked for it, sneakin' around behind Bush's back and trying to get another newspaper to toddy to him, buyin' in at the back door."

"There's been such bad stuff in the papers," Rebeccca ventured, "I've just about quit reading it. I sure can't understand it. Such name-callin'! I can't understand how Christians can get by the Almighty with such carryin'-ons and name-callin'."

"Where'd you get the idea they're good Christians?" Joshua asked.

She turned from the stove. "Why, that's easy to see. Just look at the fine houses and rich lands. They're all prosperous. With the Lord just blessing in that way, you know they're mighty pleasing to Him."

Scotty looked blankly at Joshua. "You been teaching her theology, too?"

"Not me." He turned. "Rebecca, that's about the most foolish thing I've heard you say. Fat cows and fine farms don't tell a mite about what's going on in a man's heart. Bein' in good relationship with the Lord touches the heart, not the pocketbook. I could give you a whole list of names that you'd recognize as being rich but on no account Christian. For starters, how about all those in China and India and Egypt who've never heard of the Lord?"

"Josh, me lad," Scotty drawled, "I'm a'thinkin' you'll make a much better politician than preacher. Which reminds me"—he heaved himself to his feet and reached for his hat—"mighty nice to meet you, ma'am," he bowed toward Cynthia and addressed Rebecca. "Either he ain't teachin' or you're not listenin', my dear. I'll be checking on the two of you later." Joshua followed him out the door.

Outside the pair strode rapidly toward the barn with Scotty talking all the way. "I'm serious, me lad. I'm also more'n a mite concerned. Oregon's splitting into statehood at the most difficult point in this nation's history. We need every decent, thinkin' man we can get if we're to survive in an honorable way."

Joshua took a deep breath and rounded on Scotty Mac-Lennan. "I hear you, but man, you don't understand. I love this Territory, and my heart's a'quakin' in me over the problems, but Rebecca comes first."

"Do I hear you right?"

He nodded. "She's the most important part of my life right now. When I know her to be strong and—well, then I'll be more'n eager to stick my nose into the political machinery." For a long, silent minute, Scotty was studying Joshua's face.

Slowly he said, "I get you, friend. I'm almost envying those feelings you're having. But one thing's certain"—his voice was gruff with unusual emotion—"if you can feel that way about a woman, you'll be the most compassionate governor we'll ever get." He flung himself on the horse and touched his hat.

When Joshua returned to the house, Eagle was with him,

and Joshua's shout reached Rebecca and Solali in the kitchen. "Got another plate? Eagle's back."

Just as silently as he had slipped away, Eagle had returned. And as usual, he moved in and out of the house on quiet moccasined feet. So silent and impassive was he that he seemed to Rebecca like a bronzed shadow come to life. And always his quiet, steady eyes watched Solali. Still feeling the emotion of Joshua's revelation concerning his feelings about her, using the Scripture to dig at her past, Rebecca gladly fled to Solali's problems.

First there must be a confrontation. Later, standing in their bedroom, she faced the Indian woman. "Solali, why doesn't Eagle return to his people?"

"Because he will not listen to me."

"He loves you, doesn't he? Then what are your feelings about it all?"

She turned and Rebecca was reminded that although Solali's quiet strength and even temperament seemed to belong to an older woman, she was still really only a girl.

Tormented by Joshua's words when he had, in reading the passage from Psalms, unwittingly revealed his true attitude toward her, Rebecca was conscious of the need to handle Solali's problem gently. "I don't know how your people feel about your plural marriage, but—"

Solali turned away shaking her head, "It isn't that." Then she turned back to Rebecca, frowning. "I've been reading about Jesus. He is different from the Mormon god and I am confused. They said I had to be baptized and join the church. They said I must marry a man who already had three wives. They said I must have children. I didn't have children and they were angry. Did they think I had *willed* my body to have no child?"

"But that is in the past," Rebecca said slowly. "You must put it all behind."

She shook her head. "I'm wondering what your God will demand. I—"

"Oh, no!" A cry of anguish ripped through the silent house. Momentarily Solali and Rebecca hung transfixed by the sound before Solali dashed from the room to the stairwell, with Rebecca right behind her. Together they stared down at the scene. There was Matthew. Beside him stood Cynthia holding a feebly whimpering bundle.

CHAPTER 10

Rebecca looked down on the stark white face of Matthew and understanding slowly flooded through her. She threw herself down the stairs and into Matthew's arms. Holding her childhood friend close, her tears mingled with his in shared agony.

Joshua came in from the field and Cynthia sent him down the road for Mrs. Chambers. While she rocked the tiny infant, Cynthia explained, "The Chambers have a tyke but a few months old; she'll be able to take this one on."

The story was all too familiar; no explanations were asked or given. Cynthia rocked her grandbaby while Rebecca led Matthew into the kitchen.

She knew words were impossible—for her and for him. The shock was too new. She offered only tea and embraces, a pat and more tea, this time with bread. And through it all, Rebecca was knowing herself plunged backward, thrust into a sickness of soul that she had believed impossible. Through the dull haze she bitterly assailed her false security. It was the house, Oregon, Joshua's cheerful face which had done it all. She had thought herself escaped from hell and floated to heaven—a real heaven, with no danger of hell catching up.

In the shifting patterns demanded by frontier life—the patterns that Rebecca in her emotional turmoil refused to acknowledge as ordinary life, hard and real—the household was moving quickly, adjusting. A wooden-faced Matthew took his place in the fields with the men. Motivated by hard work with the companionship of his father, brother, and the silent Indian, he was forced to live, to lay to rest the wife and companion whose body now lay beneath the soil.

During the daytime hours, Solali carried the wee one down the road to Mrs. Chambers to nurse.

The harvest was finished, the grain had been threshed, and Matthew accompanied Joshua to the Umpqua River where the grain would be ground into flour and shipped downstream to the coast.

Again Eagle disappeared, quietly, without a word. But this time his absence was brief. When he returned there was a young Indian mother and her papoose with him. His explanations were brief, and Solali interpreted with a relieved smile. "This is Kalli," she pointed to the woman; "she will stay here until Matthew's baby is weaned."

Again the household shifted. Now the commodious house seemed cramped.

When Matthew and Joshua returned, they stayed only briefly. But before they left, Joshua followed Rebecca out one evening as she carried kitchen scraps to the chickens.

Tagging along after her, he implored, "Becky, will you hear me out?" She was shaking her head. "You've refused even a word with me for the past month. Must I force you to listen? I'm just wanting to beg your pardon. But you did misunderstand me."

"You've said you wouldn't pressure me, Joshua. Keep your word."

"So be it," he muttered, and then he added, "Matthew and I will take Eagle and go up to Pa's place. He's been there alone working at that house. I suspect he'll need some help getting the roof on before the rain starts."

"Are they planning on moving before winter?"

"Yes. Could be this house will split at the seams if they don't."

"Has Matthew decided to stay?"

"Yes. When he buried his Amy he left the place for good. Says he'll never go back. Can't say that I blame him, and he's sure welcome here."

"Ah, he's about to make himself ill with it all," Rebecca said slowly, suffering over Matthew's tortured life and the tiny, motherless baby. "It would be the best thing that could happen if he would find another wife to help him with that baby." Still shaking her head, she went to toss scraps to the chickens.

"Rebecca." She heard the helpless note in his voice but shook her head. To her back he said, "Well, I'll return soon, and then you *must* listen."

She watched him walk back to the house. His square shoulders and rapid stride seemed to cancel the wistful words. There was an ache growing in her throat and she rubbed it as she watched the door close behind him. In a moment she could see a small spot of light shining through the kitchen window. He had moved the lamp in there. It was time for the Bible reading.

She sighed heavily. Why should those words Joshua had read from the Psalms matter so much to her? She lingered, taking time to scatter a handful of grain for the chickens.

When she returned to the house, she entered by the front door. Quietly she crossed the room and climbed the stairs. She dared not stay downstairs with Joshua and Matthew and the Bible reading tonight.

In the bedroom Solali was bending over the child in her lap. She gave Rebecca only a brief glance as she continued to croon to the baby as she bathed him and dressed him in clean clothing.

"What is it that you are singing to him?" Rebecca asked.

" 'Tis a Paiute lullaby, about the wind and the trees and a mother's love. Do you suppose Matthew would mind?"

"No, it's as soft as the wind itself, and the baby's nearly asleep. You really enjoy caring for little Thomas, don't you?" Solali nodded and Rebecca found herself comparing her reluctance to touch the child with Solali's obvious adoration. Solali wrapped a light blanket around the baby and lifted him to her shoulder. Rebecca followed; from the doorway of the bedroom she watched her go down the stairs, crooning and patting.

What a good mother Solali would be, even to a motherless infant! Wanting to watch that tender scene a little longer, Rebecca walked to the head of the stairs.

The stairway followed the kitchen wall down a short six steps and then turned at right angles for another six steps along the fireplace wall. The last three steps turned and bordered the massive stone fireplace. As Rebecca leaned over the railing to watch

Solali, she saw Eagle waiting on the last flight of steps.

He had been leaning against the stone of the fireplace and now he stepped into Solali's path. The lamp on the mantel illuminated Eagle's face. Solali hesitated; his expression arrested Rebecca's retreat. His soft words were Paiute, and after a moment Solali answered him in his language.

Although Rebecca had no idea what the conversation was about, she still was caught by Eagle's expression. Momentarily open, tender, it was changing as Solali spoke. In the next instant, Rebecca caught her breath. If ever she had seen a man's soul on its knees, it was now. He waited, then Solali took a backward step. Her arms about the baby tightened and her head snapped backward. There was one sharp word from her. Rebecca watched Eagle's face harden as he moved away from the light. His answer was brief, angry. Solali slipped down the stairs away from him and entered the kitchen.

Rebecca found she was holding her breath, hands clasped to her throat. The dark shadow below her moved and was gone.

Early the following morning the three of them left. Matthew and Joshua rode across the hills to their father's parcel of land. Eagle turned his horse downriver, away from them all.

Rebecca thought she was alone as she stood in the doorway and watched them ride away, but when she turned, she discovered Solali, still as ice, with her face pressed against the window.

Cynthia came from the kitchen, wiping her hands on her apron. "Are they all gone? With no menfolk to cook for today, I'm of a mind to go into town. Rebecca, you come along with me. Solali and Kalli can handle the little that needs to be done." She was removing her apron and patting her hair. "There's sewing going on at the Depoes. It's been a long time since I've had much time to gad about. I've a spot of crocheting to do, and Lettie has promised me a new pattern. You can always work on the tuckin' on that new dress." Rebecca sighed with surrender and saw Solali's amused smile as she ducked into the kitchen.

But after all was said and done, Rebecca thought, settling herself in the Depoes' parlor, it wasn't too much of a burden to poke the silly needle in and out when you had the lady-folk to take your mind off it all.

The Hanson bride was "showing" now, and for a while the talk was of babies and little knitted garments.

Mrs. Hanson, the mother-in-law of Betty Hanson, was sitting beside Rebecca. As she knitted rapidly, the pile of pink in her lap grew. "Miz Hanson," someone commented, "you know that son of yours'll have a fit when he sees that pink shawl."

"It'll not be the first boy to be wrapped in pink," she answered comfortably. "Long as the child's healthy and happy, who can complain? 'Sides, this was the only yarn I could buy. Seems everybody else hit the bunch of blue before I could get there."

"There's a pretty good crop of young'uns coming on up and down the McKenzie." The parson's wife paused to thread her needle. "And you mark my words, that's a good sign. Shows the Almighty's blessin' us all with peace and prosperity."

"Well, I'm not too certain about that." Mrs. Hanson pursed her lips. "I remember a pretty good crop being produced in the most unlikely spots. We had a bunch spread from here to there comin' across in '44. That wasn't a peace and prosperity time."

"Oh, no, it weren't," tiny Mrs. Crocket shivered. "Suffering like I'd never have believed! Comin' across I got out scot free, without losing a soul of my family, but let me tell you, that wasn't common. And 'twas but the grace of God that brought us through. If it weren't the cholera being bad enough, there was the running short of supplies. Them days there weren't no Barlow Pass or South Road to travel. We went up the Oregon Trail the whole way. When we got to The Dalles we all bunched up together in one spot. Like pourin' grain out of a narrow-necked jug, it was."

"You're talking about waiting for boats?"

Mrs. Crocket nodded. "In them days there weren't no fancy carts on railroad tracks to be pulled by mules, like they got along the river now. No sir. We had to wait to get floated down the river, and dangerous it was."

"Why were you waiting?" Rebecca asked curiously.

"Weren't enough boats to carry people," Mrs. Hanson answered.

"But the worst part of it all," Mrs. Crocket continued, "was that everybody had run out of food. We'd been livin' on mighty short rations for weeks and then there was nothing until they shipped some in from downriver."

There was a long silence in the room broken only by the occasional creak of a rocking chair. The air in the room was stifling and Rebecca rubbed at her throat.

Mrs. Crocket spoke again. "When they finally brought in supplies, some died from the shock of it."

"I don't understand," Rebecca said.

"Well, for instance, in the family camped next to us, one fella couldn't wait to cook his potatoes. He cramped up something awful and before the sun went down that night, he was dead. You can't go without food to the brink of starvation and then stuff the body without paying the consequences. No matter how hungry, you feed slow and careful or it'll do you in."

"What a terrible trick of—" Rebecca stopped. She couldn't say the word. Fate? What did that impersonal title mean? God? She dared not blame Him, yet the churning feelings were there.

During the rest of the afternoon, while the conversation shifted to a lighter tone, Rebecca found herself seething with emotion as the old questions tried to surface in her mind, tried to burst past her determination to trust God.

She found herself studying the faces of the older women. Across the room sat Mrs. Dunsberry. She had scarcely spoken all afternoon. Rebecca watched her bend over her needlework. Of all the women in the room, only she held a bright swatch of material covered with an intricate design of delicate stitchery. The other women were working on mending—repairing tiny worn garments or patching coarse homespun. Some held calico being shaped into new garments or woolen yarn being furiously knit in a race against winter.

Rebecca's attention was drawn back to Marsella Dunsberry. She studied her face, her dainty dress, and the carefully coiffed hair. It was like looking at a china doll with very sad features. Cynthia leaned close and whispered, "She's a strange one, but there's reasons. Lost her husband and two children movin' west. Most strange it is that she stays."

Briefly Mrs. Dunsberry lifted her head and looked at Rebecca. When she picked up her needlework again, not a flicker of expression had marred her face.

Wonderingly, Rebecca turned to study Mrs. Hanson and Mrs.

Crocket. Their tales had given the somber note to the afternoon, and Mrs. Hanson didn't conceal her heartache but had talked freely about the loss of two of her children. Yet both women were serene of face and composure. The little Mrs. Crocket seemed impossibly small and frail, but she had talked about wrestling the oxen and heavy wagon across the desert while her sick husband tossed with fever. Even now, her face was as smooth as if she had never experienced a worry in her life. Watching her laugh and smile as she mended torn trousers, Rebecca couldn't help sighing as she picked up her own sewing.

Mrs. Hanson was watching her, and Rebecca's words tumbled out. "I'm begging the sense to understand all this. Seems the trials you and Mrs. Crocket have lived through would have beat you under, but you're acting and talking as if it was all to be expected."

Mrs. Hanson frowned, "But it *was*." She shifted the yarn and said thoughtfully, "Not a one of us really believed in our hearts when we left home that we'd follow our men clear across those plains without suffering. Sure, we loved them, and sure, there were many more good days than bad. I suppose that's what kept us going."

"The love for your husbands?"

"No, more'n that." She paused and her brow wrinkled again. "My, I don't suppose I've ever paused long enough in my whole life to try to put it all into words. But, then, the feeling's the important thing. Even if you can't understand the pain being served up when you've set your heart on nothing but good, you're still believing that the Almighty loves you and is sittin' right there with His eyes on you, ready and willin' to help you. It's that kind of knowing that gets you through, not all the questions that you can drag up that there's no answer for."

CHAPTER 11

" 'The Lord *is* my shepherd.' " The words seemed as dry as dust, but Rebecca read doggedly. While Solali held the baby close, Cynthia curiously studied them both.

It was impulse that had prompted Rebecca to carry her Bible down the stairs this evening, the first evening since the men had all departed. At the time the impulse had seemed right. But now as she closed the Book and folded her hands for prayer, her courage faltered.

"Seems a body gets enough of that at church every Sunday without having to spend time at it during the week." Cynthia got to her feet with a snort. Reaching for the baby she said, "Here, I'll carry him to Kalli and then tuck him in." Solali surrendered him reluctantly.

Her parting shot was delivered from the door. "And you, Solali, ought to be getting your own babies. Like Kalli. I'm seein' how you hunger after my grandson."

Solali's eyes widened as Cynthia headed for the stairs. Hastily Rebecca said, "Don't mind her, Solali. Age has sharpened her tongue somewhat."

" 'Tis no wonder Kalli spends most of her time upstairs."

Rebecca was still fingering the Bible when Cynthia came back into the room. The woman watched Solali get to her feet and leave before she turned to Rebecca. "And you, young lady, I've seen the way my son looks at you. I'm guessing he'll not be content until you marry him. But I'm also thinking that things will be better for us all when we come right out and say what's on our minds."

"Cynthia," Rebecca whispered, guessing the questions she wanted to ask, those which had darkened and narrowed her eyes for months. "I can't talk about it, please."

"I know." Briefly compassion gentled her voice, and when Rebecca looked up, she watched the dark questioning in Cynthia's eyes lift—just for a moment. But Rebecca knew those eyes were really seeing her, looking beyond the surface as she said, "I'm as sharp as any old biddy, trying to guess all the details. Before God and man, can you say that my son knows what he's getting into?"

She could only nod, but the hand at her throat felt the heavy beat of her pulse.

Cynthia released her breath in an explosion of sound. "I won't pretend that I don't have my doubts and my questions, but I'll give you a fair chance. You know there's plenty of talk that's come out of *that* place." She waited and when Rebecca didn't answer, she said, "Seein' he's made up his mind, well, then, the sooner the better."

"Cynthia, I'm not ready. I'm not certain that ever—" She pressed her hand against her mouth and swallowed hard. The word had been *again*. Now the word swirled through her mind, searing with all its implications. Little did Cynthia know the real thrust of Joshua's thoughts or her own.

There were those other words of King David, the ones after Psalm 23, reminding Rebecca of Joshua's true feelings, of how he really saw her. "Purge me with hyssop, and I shall be clean . . ." and, "Thou shalt not . . ." Did Joshua really think the hyssop would take away the thrust of those other thoughts? *Adultery. Fallen woman.*

She watched Cynthia move about the kitchen, making the nighttime preparations for the next day that were so familiar. She set the crushed wheat to soak and stirred flour into her bread sponge. Lifting the clean dish towels, she folded them and placed them on the shelf beside the stove. She took the dipper from the pail and drank deeply of the water. Now with a brisk nod to Rebecca, she murmured, "Good night."

Rebecca was still staring at the blue bowl on the table when she heard the whisper of Solali's moccasins. She walked into the circle of light and sat down at the table.

As Rebecca studied the Indian woman, a strange mixture of feelings went through her. At one moment she saw her as Indian and completely without understanding of the white man's way of life, then she was caught in a moment when their spirits seemed linked, when they were filled with the common memories of the past. At those times she knew Solali wiser than herself. There was that serene acceptance of life, at least outwardly, when Rebecca knew so little serenity.

She must probe. "Solali, about the Bible. Do you understand now that I must follow Jesus?"

A tiny frown marred her forehead. "You say this Jesus is God come to live among us and to die for us to satisfy the demands of an angry God." She waved her hand in frustration, "No, no, that's all wrong. I still struggle. I know the Mormon god is angry, he punishes disobedience and withholds good so that we will obey him. Never will we be good enough, because he blesses with good and plenty when we are righteous enough. And we are poor—that means"; she paused, shrugged, and then said, "Most of the Indian gods are angry too. They must be appeased. They say there are good gods, but I don't know any. Now this Book tells me about the death of the good man who was really God and what He does is not to please an angry God but instead to clear the path to a righteous God." She stopped and sighed. "It is too heavy for my mind. I cannot understand it all."

Rebecca was whispering but her thoughts were not so much for Solali as for herself. She said, " 'For God so loved the world, that he gave his only begotten Son, that whosoever believeth in him should not perish, but have everlasting life.' "

"Then God is—" Solali shivered, a puzzled expression in her eyes, as she tried to explain her feelings. "It's so far beyond what I've heard. I think I need to read more in the Book. It is so hard to remember it all."

"That's why Joshua wants us to read every night."

"The words"—now it was Solali who was whispering—"they are holy, if they are from the Great Father, as you say. If so, we dare not forget one of them." She lifted her hands, cupped in supplication. For one brief moment, Rebecca caught the awe Solali was feeling. She felt her heart respond and lift in adoration. Then silence dropped into her soul. She sighed and stood up.

The two left the kitchen together and walked up the stairs to their bedroom. From across the hall came the sleepy whimper of Matthew's baby and the answering murmur from Kalli.

As Rebecca settled herself to sleep, she said, " 'Tis a lonely house without the menfolk. I'm glad we have neighbors close enough to run to."

"You're thinking Indians?"

Reluctantly, "Doesn't the mind go that way when one's alone?"

Through the silence of the night, Solali said slowly, "They call us savages and say we must learn the white man's ways. If I follow your God, then I best marry a white man, isn't that so?"

Rebecca raised herself to one elbow and stared over at the dusky face. "Solali, I don't recollect reading anything in the Bible that leads me to think that way. Why do you?" The dark head moved restlessly on the pillow but there was no answer.

Ten days later, as Rebecca worked alone in the garden, she reflected on the activities that occupied the women's time while the men were gone. Despite the busy hours, there was an emptiness, a waiting. Suddenly a scream pierced her lonely thoughts. Rebecca pitched her armload of weeds and ran toward the house.

The screaming was coming from the kitchen, from Kalli's child. She burst through the kitchen door and stopped in amazement. Solali was holding a frothing mass of flying arms and legs, trying to submerge it in the washtub. Hair tumbled, soaked, Solali lifted her face. "Rebecca, help! This child thinks I'm trying to drown him."

Kalli stood beside the stove. Her dark eyes were filled with apprehension as she looked from Rebecca to the child, but she made no move to rescue her frantic son. Reluctantly Rebecca knelt beside the tub and tried to grasp the thrashing arms.

"Ho, ho!" the booming voice filled the room and the thrashing ceased. It was Matthew filling the doorway. Kalli flew to him and Solali settled back on her heels and pushed the hair out of her eyes.

"Oh, Matthew," Rebecca jumped to her feet and embraced him. "You're back."

"And just in time. What are you two trying to do to the young man?" He picked up the towel and lifted the child. "There, young fella. This always happens when the women outrank us men." While his jovial voice rumbled contentedly, the child cuddled against him.

Matthew continued to rub the child and Rebecca studied his face. The lines of unhappiness seemed to have lifted. "You're bone thin," she accused; "I suppose you've all been working yourselves night and day and living on scraps."

He nodded. "Need to get the place finished before the rains start. Josh stayed to help Pa finish up. He'll be along next week." Matthew reached for the little clothes Kalli held out.

With an exasperated sigh, Solali ruefully surveyed the messy scene and said, "Law, it sure would help to talk whatever language she speaks."

Matthew put the tot on his feet and turned to lift the tub of water. "If you ladies had just turned him loose in the crick, he'd have got almost as clean and there'd be no call for the fussin'." His voice was still the contented rumble, and he followed Solali out the door with the tub.

Cynthia came into the kitchen with an armload of freshly dried sheets. Shaking her head at the rumpled towel and the pool of water on the floor, she dumped her load on the table and reached for a dry towel. She nodded toward the door. "I'm beginning to think that Matthew's gone soft on Solali. Just my lot to have a flock of Indians for grandbabies."

Surprised, Rebecca turned to look through the open door. Matthew and Solali stood beside the garden patch talking earnestly. Slowly Rebecca said, "I think you're jumping to conclusions." But she remembered that statement Solali had made, and Eagle's face. His tenderness had changed to bitter disappointment in response to Solali's words.

Just after supper that evening, the wind gusted through the valley bringing cool air and a swirl of rain. While the women were finishing the dishes, Matthew knelt beside the fireplace and said, "Let's have a fire and read the Bible here."

Rebecca came to the doorway to look at him. Her thoughts were busy with pictures of Matthew at Bible-reading time in the past. His disinterest and sorrow seemed to leave no room to hear and respond to the words of comfort and help which Joshua had chosen to read.

The fire was blazing. Matthew crossed the big room and entered Joshua's bedroom. When he returned he was carrying Joshua's Bible.

"Oh," Solali said slowly. She was standing in the doorway to the kitchen holding Rebecca's Bible. "Then you won't need this one." She came to sit on the settle with Rebecca. Kalli came into the room carrying the baby. She hesitated, then sat on a stool close to the fire and cuddled the child.

A wistful expression crept across Matthew's countenance as he looked down into his son's face. "I'd be obliged if he favors his ma," he said slowly.

His hand was trembling as he opened the Bible. "I guess I'd better tell you that I've made my peace with God." His voice was self-conscious and he fumbled with the Book. "Josh made me see, no matter what, the most important thing isn't understanding but *trusting* God." A quick finger rubbed at his eyes and a folded paper slipped from the pages of the Book.

Rebecca picked up the paper and shoved it into her Bible. Her heart was heavy with its answer to Matthew's sorrow. "Ah, Matt, we know. 'Tis a sorry lot trying to outguess God."

When the others had slipped away to their beds, Rebecca continued to sit beside the fire.

Matthew's confessions had released the tide of thought which she kept dammed up in the back of her mind. Now the dark clouds of memory surfaced and set her hands trembling and dabbing at the tears. Impatiently she moved quickly and opened her Bible, seeking the solace of the words. The familiar ones, the comforting ones.

Instead, she found the paper from Joshua's Bible. She started up with it, then realized that Matthew had carried Joshua's Bible back into the room with him. The door was closed and the house silent with sleeping people.

While her fingers fumbled with the paper, she realized it was a letter addressed to her. "Dear Rebecca," she read. "Seems I express myself best on paper. I've no call to apologize, for I was offering you the best from my heart with the insights His Spirit gave me. That I've hurt you, there is no doubt, and for that I apologize. It seems I was bringing out thoughts from His Word that were new to you. I was never guessing that you didn't see what seemed both natural and clear to me. I'm understanding now. I've been hearing men talk about God's Word truly and honestly. I'm convinced that the loving Heavenly Father has provided everything for us that we need through the blessed atonement of Jesus Christ. Now I'm guessing you've not seen how far His loving care goes in restoring us to himself."

Rebecca dropped the letter to her lap. Joshua's tender words unleashed a torrent, and she began recalling the words Joshua had read to her. " 'Restore unto me the joy of thy salvation' ." Even as she whispered the words, she wondered what they really meant.

She went back to the letter. "Little Becky," she read, "I've been seeing you moving into a darkness of spirit, and His words burn through me. I'm not understanding it all, but I read in the Bible that those lashes the Romans put on Him counted for something. In Isaiah it says that by His stripes we are healed. I can't help remembering the way He touched the people while He walked this earth, healing them from one end of the fellow to the other. I've been praying for that poor, injured side of yours. One of these days, I'm going to tell you what I'll be doing about that wound. Right now I count it a blessing when I see you kneading the bread and using the broom, even while I know it hurts. But isn't it right to think He can take away all those black memories you have?"

She dropped the letter to her lap again and stared into the dying fire. Her fingers crept to her side and traced the tender furrow of scar tissue. As the wind lashed the trees and drove the rain against the house, Rebecca's thoughts drifted.

On a long-ago night, in her lonesomeness, she had wished for the kind of soul-deep communication that Joshua was now offering to her. She winced, feeling again the pain his quote from David had brought, the picture of shame they had drawn.

"Times like these," she muttered, "makes a body want to fly back to where there's no taint." She stopped, stunned by a sudden realization. "Just like the children of Israel," she whispered, "things get bad, and you're yearning for the leeks and garlic of Egypt."

She shivered and poked another stick on the fire. With the need to defend herself, she muttered, "Well, 'tis a barren land where people see you different than you are." Now she picked up her Bible. "Might as well read; there's no sleeping on a lonesome night like this." Briefly her thoughts dwelt on Joshua. Was he sheltered from the rain? Was he eating enough?

Moving restlessly on the hard wooden settle that bordered the fireplace, Rebecca slowly turned the pages of the Bible. Occasionally she paused to read, snatching at words which now caught her attention and then became lost as the storm outside grew in intensity.

She started up from her seat. Almost she thought her mind was playing fancies, that there had been a voice and the sound of hooves against stone. Now above the pounding of the rain there was the unmistakable crash of the barn door. She ran to the kitchen window. At the moment she caught sight of movement outside and as she turned to shout for Matthew, the door crashed inward. Joshua and his father stumbled into the room.

Clutching her throat, she stared at their dripping figures. "It's raining up the way," Joshua explained, reaching for towels. "Pa and I decided we'd come home for some hot grub." Around the towel, beyond the lightness of his words, his eyes were full of concern. While Mr. Smyth rubbed his head and started for the stairs, Joshua asked, "You all right?"

She sighed and dropped her hand. Turning abruptly she poked kindling into the stove. He touched her shoulder, "I've frightened you. Becky, I'm sorry. Seems everything I do goes awry."

"It's just—" she gulped, fighting the feeling which had sent her heart to pounding. Her hands trembled against the towels. "I hadn't expected you."

"I was getting uneasy, thinking of the things that needed to be done here. When the rain started, Pa and I decided to come. There's no likelihood of getting shingling done in this weather."

She watched him cross the parlor to the bedroom where Matthew was sleeping. Still conscious of the new rush of warmth and life his coming had brought, she began taking down plates and cups. She was lifting bacon and eggs from the frying pan and stacking buttered toast on its warming plate when the two men came into the kitchen. Wearing dry clothes but still shivering, they sat down while she poured tea into their cups.

"We'd a' had the place completely shingled if the weather'd held," Mr. Smyth said as he took his cup and gulped the hot liquid.

Looking at the food, Joshua added, "Yes, but we'd a' starved to death beforehand."

Rebecca was finishing up the dishes and setting the kitchen in order when she heard the stairs creak. She looked to the door and Mr. Smyth said, "Night, Becky, and thanks." She nodded. In the parlor Joshua was pushing a log into the cracking fire. She turned back to the kitchen. The rain still pounded at the window. Slowly she wiped the table and hung the wet towels.

From the doorway Joshua said, "I see you found my letter."

"It fell out of the Bible when Matt was getting ready to read. It had my name on it so—"

"Don't get your back up. I intended for you to see it some time. Will you listen to me now?"

His broad shoulders filled the doorway. There would be no pushing past him. She clung to the back of the chair, filled with a new consciousness of him. The times he had held her, helped her, carried her; feeding, touching, urging life back into her at the worst of it as they had fled across Utah Territory.

Now she realized that, trusting as a child, she had known only a child's emotional response to him. But it was changing. At what moment had it happened? What thought or need, what event, plunged her toward this understanding? Was it the feeling of unending vigilance as he had cared for her? Was it his strength, surrounding her, demanding response and life when life seemed impossible? Was it that man on the mountain, the woodcutter, stripped of his shirt, revealing the gold ring shining against his golden body? Rebecca shook her head—slowly, wearily, unknowing and confused.

"Why? Will you run forever?" She tried to reply and the words were lost, but the theme of them was in her thoughts: unworthy.

He lifted her hand from the back of the chair and led her to the settle, saying, in that gentle, companionable way of his, "Upstairs we've a heap of feathers just waiting to be made into cushions for this thing."

He leaned against the fireplace and gazed down into the crackling fire. "About that from Psalms. At the time I read those words to you, Becky, I'd no idea you'd see me as judging you. Rebecca, you've told me yourself how you're trusting in the atonement of Jesus Christ, saying you've accepted His forgiveness for—" the word hung unsaid. Now he added, "Then do you think I'd *dare* judge you? I was trying to say to you the words I've heard preached a good many times, how a person must *let* God. He'll not only forgive sins forever, but He'll begin changing him into a new person." He stopped to take a deep breath before saying, "He wants you to be rid of the past and able to live the future with love for everyone."

"Love!" Rebecca cried, her mind spiraling down into that black pool of memory. "You mean that I am to love—" With a quick movement Joshua was beside her, his fingers pressed against her lips.

"Don't say it," he demanded sternly. "I'm seeing you changed now. Listen." He released her and settled back on his heels beside the fireplace. Slowly quoting Isaiah he said, " ' . . . he hath sent me to bind up the brokenhearted, to proclaim liberty to the captives, and the opening of the prison to them that are bound . . . to comfort all that mourn . . . to give unto them beauty for ashes, the oil of joy for mourning, the garment of praise for the spirit of heaviness . . . that he might be glorified.' Rebecca." He was whispering now. "Those verses are talking about Jesus Christ and what He wants to do in people's lives. That's what I'm wanting for you."

CHAPTER 12

Beauty for ashes. The little white church was quiet, waiting. Slowly the congregation filed in. In the Smyth family pew Rebecca was seated beside Solali, who was in church for the first time. Rebecca kept looking at her, admiring the new calico dress and the smooth cap of dark hair, fashioned like Rebecca's sunlit locks. Matthew was sitting beside her holding his infant son. The brooding expression on his face told his story. Beside him sat Cynthia, and her straying fingers straightened the blanket, touched the downy head. Mr. Smyth was beside his wife. While the years had softened her figure and sharpened her tongue, the years on Mr. Smyth had served only to wither and warp. Next were Jamie and his intended, Eva, whose adoring eyes were fixed on the slight man beside her.

Rebecca watched the pair. This was the first time Jamie had been home since Becky had arrived in Oregon. She seemed unable to fill her eyes with enough of the young man who was a smaller version of Joshua. He caught her eye and smiled. Beauty for ashes. This was beauty.

The young man in cutaways strode across the platform and seated himself at the organ. There were the opening chords and the nod of his head. The congregation stood and sang: "Praise God, from whom all blessings flow—Praise Him, all creatures . . ."

The sun streamed through the high, bare windows. She could see clouds and sky, branches and birds. Beauty.

The jangle of harness and the creak of a wagon wheel momentarily overwhelmed the Parson's voice. Beauty.

Beauty was the present, ashes the past. The ashes still lay heavy upon Rebecca's heart, stirred now and again as a sensation of life tried to creep beyond the pain of the past.

She was wishing she could remember all those other words Joshua had read to her. She clung to the Book in her lap and wished she dared to search for the words now.

After the meeting, the grounds were dotted with tables and benches and friendly groups. As before, during the summer months, the valley dwellers had carried their dinner to church. While the afternoon slipped away, the best of the settlement's cooking was shared.

Today Rebecca sat at the picnic table and listened to the chatter about her. Did these people know their lives were being cemented as surely as the icing held Mrs. Hanson's cake together?

She saw Kalli sitting under a tree nursing the baby and watched her dark eyes shift from one group to another. Her impassive face didn't reflect a single thought or hint of emotion. She seemed unaware of the tiny blonde boy at her breast. What magic had Eagle worked to bring this timid creature into Matthew's life to serve as wet nurse for his child?

But Kalli was a woman, like Rebecca. She was separated by culture and language and surrounded by strangeness, unable to communicate with those around her; Rebecca was seeing her as another pattern of herself.

In the merrymaking about the tables, Kalli was forgotten. A feeling of helplessness turned Rebecca restless in the presence of those dark eyes. Jumping to her feet, Rebecca selected a piece of fried chicken from the platter and went toward Kalli.

Kneeling beside the woman, she saw Kalli's son curled on the corner of his mother's robe. He was asleep, a piece of bread clutched in his hand, his cheeks streaked with dust and tears.

Kalli nodded as she took the chicken and nibbled at it. Rebecca's feelings were spilling over. "Oh, Kalli," she whispered, knowing the woman didn't understand, "I wish I could help; yet you came voluntarily."

A calico skirt stopped beside Rebecca and Solali folded her

legs under the billowing skirt and sat beside Kalli. "It's a fear-some feeling to not be able to say the words," she said. "I know. I can no more speak her language than you. Eagle says her husband is dead and she was unhappy in the lodge of her husband's family. I'm feeling in time she'll become one of us."

Rebecca studied Solali's troubled face. "Are you meaning someone like yourself who has chosen a new life?" Solali nodded and turned her face away.

The woman sat in silence until finally, with a sigh of futility, Rebecca started to rise. Softly Solali said, "If I could speak to her, I would make her realize it is worse to belong to two worlds. The heart never leaves home."

Rebecca paused. "Why don't you have Eagle tell her this?" Startled, Solali's head snapped backward and she stared up at Rebecca. The movement reminded Rebecca of the scene at the bottom of the stairs when in just this way Solali had looked up at Eagle. Solali's eyes were pools of misery. Slowly she shook her head.

Rebecca walked back to the table while the two Indian women continued to sit under the tree. It was the first time, Rebecca realized, as she watched Solali, that she had seen her friend choose to act in a manner contrary to the image of the white woman.

A yellow leaf dropped from the tree overhead and landed on Rebecca's plate. Nettie Morgan said, "September's snuggin' close. Then comes winter and the rains begin. 'Tis a good season for the women to go a'visitin'. You come." For a moment curiosity gleamed in her eyes. "You know, for all the time you've been here, we scarcely know you. Cynthia's told us a little about how she came to know you and all, but she's pretty close-mouthed. Almost mysterious-like. Seems to think if there's to be any gettin' acquainted, you best be informing us. Says you've been a schoolteacher." There was a pause and then, "Seems there's always a call for good teachers around about. Now, when we get to be a state and there's aid from Washington, there'll be more call for teachers and new schools."

Now she turned to watch Solali get to her feet. "Think that Indian will be marrying Matthew?"

Rebecca pointed to the next table where Cynthia and a young woman were talking. "I'm thinking Cynthia has other ideas. That girl's a pretty little thing, but she doesn't look more'n fourteen." The woman was still watching Solali and Rebecca was remembering the phrase, *the heart never leaves home.*

Rebecca turned slowly, "This Waltstown is a nice little place. Seems every time I look there's a new store or house being built."

"Have you been in Madame Tuchey's shop? It's advertised in the newpapers even. Says she does dressmakin' and hats. But I'm a'guessing she'll have to find another occupation to keep goin' in backwoods country like this."

The woman snickered and Rebecca looked at her. "You're implying she's not nice." Rebecca saw her smirk and bite her lip before adding, "You're just guessing?"

The woman flushed, "Pretty obvious, ain't it? Us frontier women haven't the money to support the likes of a hat shop."

"But there's a new organ in the church. I'm thinking it's short supply that limits the people more'n money." Rebecca continued to study the woman and her thoughts were busy, placing her own name under the innuendo. Abruptly Nettie got to her feet and began gathering her dishes. Her cheeks were red as she impatiently settled her basket and called her daughter.

"Mrs. Morgan," Rebecca began with a sinking heart.

"Not now!" she snapped. "I'll be talkin' to you later." Her skirt swished as she marched off.

Cynthia handed Rebecca a basket. "Take this to the wagon. And, Becky, I'd be of a mind to step softly around Nettie Morgan. Maybe 'tis gossip, but you haven't a call to sweeten her tongue."

Rebecca's ears were still burning as she crawled into the wagon and turned to watch Solali and Kalli. Solali's unhappy face made it clear there was only one thing to do. "That Eagle," she muttered, "I do wish he would learn to speak and *understand* English."

Joshua looked down at her and said, "Maybe he knows more English than you've guessed, and maybe he knows the best way to avoid woman chatter is by pretendin' otherwise." His eyes were dancing and she guessed that he had heard the whole silly conversation with Mrs. Morgan.

Cynthia heaved herself into the wagon and said, "Joshua, I'd be inclined to use your wagon tomorrow. Rebecca and Solali could be takin' a load up to the house. Now the roof's tight there's no reason we can't be movin' things slow and easy-like."

"Ma, I've never seen you do anything slow and easy-like," Joshua teased, "and I'm thinking you want to jaw Pa about finishing up the place. He's hurryin'."

The next day Rebecca and Solali took the wagon and team up the road to the elder Smyth's section. The trip in the ponderous wagon, behind the plodding horses, took all of the forenoon. But, then, the precarious load didn't lend itself to faster travel. There was the chest of quilts and cases of dishes and canning jars. Mrs. Smyth's rocking chair insisted on rocking, and the little footstool and the tall clothes horse kept colliding. Solali played referee and grumbled.

" 'Tis a pity she couldn't wait for the men to pack this wagon properly. They'd have been through with plowing that section by evening."

"But isn't this a lark!" Rebecca exclaimed.

"Lark?" Solali asked suspiciously.

"A—a happiness." Rebecca scrambled for words. Once in a while she hit a snag in Solali's understanding and then she was doubly conscious of her friend's Indian heritage. Looking at Solali, she asked, "Did Eagle say when he would be back?"

There was the lifted chin. "No, and I didn't encourage him to return at all."

They turned off the road and wound down the trail to the house. The Smyths' new house sat in the sprawl of older buildings and corrals which had been constructed years before when the section was first claimed under the Donation Land Act.

When Solali pointed to the older buildings with a frown, Rebecca explained, "At the time Joshua brought his family to Oregon Territory, his pa made his claim up here and worked the land, but they built Joshua's large home and all lived there together."

"And the Ma and Pa are moving because of us?"

"No, Joshua said they'd already decided to make this move. Two years ago. It's taken that long to get the house built, with helping Joshua and all." Her voice trailed away. Again she was deeply conscious of the sacrifice Joshua had made in order to find her. Now she saw how his search had affected the whole family.

The trail ended in front of the little house. The aroma of newness and fresh lumber still clung to it, and the planed wood shone bright and clean. " 'Tis almost too pretty to cover up with white paint," Rebecca said, pointing to the golden wood.

"Those windowpanes are in need of a good scrubbing," Solali observed.

"Oh, that'll wait. It's the push to get the roof completed and the paint on before the rains start."

"After the desert country it seems a marvel to worry about a whole season of rain, doesn't it?" Solali slid down from the wagon seat and turned to Rebecca. "Are you hurting? I was hard pressed to not complain about her sending you off like this when I was guessing your poor side screamed with pain."

"It did hurt," Rebecca admitted as she went to turn the horses loose to graze. "I've just got to act otherwise. Cynthia would have been full of questions if a big strapping girl like me couldn't heft a little chest of drawers like this without complaining."

"Just the same"—Solali gave Rebecca a push—"you let me do the lifting now and you just ease it to the ground. I 'spect Joshua will fuss when he finds what she's put you through today."

"He'll not say a word," Rebecca said shortly.

It was on the return trip that Rebecca accepted the changes in her life. Solali had been talking about how Cynthia's furnishings would fit into the little home, when Rebecca began thinking of the gaps that were being created in Joshua's home.

She was standing in the parlor later, looking around at the empty spaces in Joshua's house when Cynthia came into the room. "It does look bare without my rocker and the fancy work around. I 'spect you'll get yourself busy with such things this winter. The women visit around with their fancy work and they'll be asking you to join. I don't know about Solali. But if she's going to be a white man's wife, she'll need to be learnin' too."

Solali was hesitating in the doorway to the kitchen. Her face was troubled and she turned away. Rebecca was so full of wondering about that expression that Cynthia's words didn't immediately catch her attention.

But now Cynthia was addressing her. "What about you? It's going to be a bad spot you'll be in if he marries her and they all move back up Salem way. He'll be needing Kalli for another year, so that leaves you and Joshua here."

She marched past Rebecca and entered Joshua's bedroom. Rebecca went to the kitchen to find Solali. "Did you hear her? Is that what you intend?"

Solali was standing beside the table and she turned, puzzled. "Rebecca, I—"

Cynthia came back into the room. "I saw these old newspapers in a stack in Joshua's room. They're just the thing I need to wrap these jars of fruit."

"Oh." Rebecca looked down at the table. "I'd not noticed you'd been cleaning out the fruit closet while we were gone."

"The menfolk'll be going up that way soon and if I've packed a box or two real good with these newspapers around the jars, well, then they can carry the batch without breaking 'em."

Rebecca pulled the wooden crate close to the table and said, "We'd better be at it. 'Tis getting close to suppertime."

Solali picked up a newspaper and shook out the folds while Cynthia immediately went back to her former topic. "Now, Becky, folks are asking about your intentions already. What's a body to say with Josh tellin' me to keep my words to myself?"

Solali lowered the paper. There was a touch of strain in her voice as she asked, "Where did you get these papers?"

"In Joshua's bedroom. They's old ones."

Solali glanced quickly at Rebecca and said, "I'm a'wondering if he'll want you to use them—there's, well—" she stopped and looked imploringly at Rebecca.

Mystified, Rebecca reached for a paper, "What is it, Solali?" But Solali held the paper away from Rebecca. As she opened her mouth to speak, Cynthia snatched one of the papers from the stack and turned to the window.

"Oh, oh," she muttered, "this 'uns got an article in it that bodes no good for the Mormons. I don't read too good, but leastwise I can understand this."

"Joshua's been saving these for a purpose; we'd best put them back," Rebecca said hastily.

"No, not until I've read a bit more." Cynthia's voice was full of suspicion, and the glance she threw Rebecca's way made her heart sink. Now Solali gasped and Cynthia reached for her paper. "Read it to me or I'll figure it out for myself." Solali was shaking her head. Backing away from Cynthia, she tried to hold the paper away from her.

The back door flew open and Joshua came through. His easy grin disappeared as he looked from his mother to the jars and the newspapers and then to Solali's outstretched arm.

"I see you've found my newspapers," he said slowly as he looked at his mother.

"Just a bunch of old ones, I thought. I'd have never believed otherwise since I don't read well, but Solali here was gasping over them like they's pretty good. So's I'll just be reading them for myself if I can't get Solali to read them for me."

Slowly Solali lowered her arm and held the newspaper toward Joshua. With a sigh, Joshua took the paper and placed it back on the stack. When Cynthia reached for it, he said, "No, Ma. If you insist, I'll tell you what they have to say. And I expect when I'm done, you'll be none the happier or the wiser."

"Then why've you been hangin' onto them all this time?" Cynthia snapped. "I already saw they're old. Some's from California and there's more from Oregon, but they came out in the year 1852. We weren't even here then. How come you have them?"

"I've made it a point to keep up on the things going on in Utah Territory. These are the tales that have come out of there."

"But are they truth?" Solali asked softly.

Joshua turned toward her. "Only the good Lord knows for certain, Solali, but I'm certain there's a pretty good basis for the stories, otherwise they wouldn't keep a'flowin' out of the Territory."

"What do they say?" Cynthia demanded.

Joshua picked up the paper Solali had returned to him. "This fellow is quoting an emigrant who had the misfortune of hesitating too long in Mormon country. A great deal of this is reprinted from a pamphlet, probably written by either a Mr. Slater or a Mr. Goodell. At the beginning the fella is quoting a judge in Utah Territory. It's his remarks to the Gentiles during a trial. He says that he is thanking God that in the time not far distant he'll have the authority to pass sentence of life and death upon the Gentiles, and that he intends to have their heads snatched like a chicken being readied for the pot. Then the fella writing goes on to repeat a few words from Brigham Young. The gentleman quotes Brigham Young as saying that if a Gentile says anything against the Mormons, they'll take off their heads—in spite of all the emigrants and the United States and all hell, that'll be done."

He lowered the paper. "Now, Ma, you any wiser or happier?"

"Wiser," she muttered slowly, looking at Rebecca. "But read the rest; I want to know it all."

"No, Ma. You can see there's a fair stack here. Some's letters written to the newspapers by overlanders who've suffered at the hands of the people of Utah Territory, and it's not going to do you a bit of good to hear it all. I had to know what was going on until I could get Rebecca out of the place." His voice softened. "She's here. Now's the time to help her rebuild a life that's been hurt terrible by those years in the Territory. Ma, your place is just to love Rebecca. She's safe; let her forget about the place."

Cynthia lifted her chin. "Leastwise, how do I know she's not here to spread their ways?" Rebecca gave a weak cry of protest, but Joshua's hand was restraining her.

"No more, Ma. You have no idea what Rebecca's suffered through and it'll be her secret forever. You've no right to pry. Rebecca's no more a threat to you than I am. We both serve the same Lord. Now, please, hush forever about it all."

Cynthia hesitated and Rebecca saw her tightly pursed lips. Her heart sank even more as she saw Joshua relax and smile at his mother. With a shrug Cynthia slowly reached for the papers. "Well, no call to waste them; I'll just use them to wrap the jars like I intended all along."

"No, Ma." Joshua was still smiling as he scooped up the papers. He stuffed them into the stove and struck a match. In silence they stood in the kitchen and listened to the roar of flames.

"I wish the matter could be settled forever with so little fuss," Solali said slowly as she turned and walked from the room.

CHAPTER 13

The next evening, after supper, Joshua said, "Matt and I'll be leaving in the morning. I've cut the last of the hay and mended the barn. There's enough wood to do for a time. Now we'll get Pa's place tight for the winter. A week up there ought to finish it all."

"Then you'll come get the rest of my furniture," Cynthia said with satisfaction.

"And I'll be facing a pretty bare house," Joshua remarked. "About time I take Rebecca and Solali up Salem way to buy some furniture for this place."

The baby fretted, and words were passed around the table as casually as the pot of stew. Rebecca realized she was staring at Joshua and she tried to force her attention back to her plate. But the thought of traveling to Salem, going into those big shops and selecting furniture for this house—Joshua's house—filled her mind. She was seeing wood—polished, carved, just like the MacLennans'. A table, chairs, a sideboard materialized in her thoughts. She felt Joshua's silence and glanced at him.

His presence across the table from her was overwhelming. The open neck of his shirt revealed the slender rawhide thong. She watched the muscles across his shoulders ripple as he passed the pitcher of milk. Now he looked up at her and the force of his blue eyes was boring into hers, demanding an answer for a question not yet asked. He would never be like his pa, shooed with the broom of a busy housewife, relegated to his corner, used impatiently, tolerated. Joshua was not to be ignored.

114

Her hand slipped upward to her throat and she was remembering the way he had looked that night before the fireplace. While the rain had battered the house, she had felt his eyes boring into her soul. Could he see into the very bottom of her thoughts? Would a man whose strength and wisdom stemmed from the God whose black Book he held be a presence she could live with for the rest of her life? She trembled.

Joshua looked at the hand gripping her throat, and she saw the questions in his eyes.

Later, after supper, Solali was alone in the kitchen. The dishes had been washed and dried. She was hanging the towels when Matthew came into the kitchen. She felt his constraint before he said, "Solali, come walk down to the river with me. It's a pretty night and Josh said the fish are jumpin'." Her fingers slowly stroked the towels.

When she finally turned to look into his face, all the easy answers she had dreamed of saying fled away. "Yes, Matthew, I'll go if you want."

They walked toward the McKenzie. Here the river tumbled out of the mountains and the force of it had created a hard bed for the cataracts. In giant steps it plunged down the valley as it rushed to join the twisting Willamette, combining to wash through the valley toward the Columbia River.

As Matthew and Solali walked through the thickets of berry bushes and willow on a path cut by others, Solali was thinking of the young married couples in the valley, those who had obviously used this path to good advantage in the past. There was a sadness beginning in her heart, and she knew now was the time to face herself honestly. Life would be much different than what she had dreamed of since coming to the Oregon Territory. One look at Matthew's face tonight had revealed this.

Matthew's words interrupted her thoughts. "You like the little tyke, don't you? I've been watching you. My little fella needs a mother."

"I am Indian."

"But different than Kalli. We don't even speak her language."

"She will learn."

"Solali, you've been raised by white people." He stopped and then said, "Aw, Solali, it doesn't even matter if you have two heads. I want to marry you."

She faced him in the dusk. "Until this evening I wanted to marry you. But—" How could she ignore all his yearning face revealed, and how could she hurt him by admitting the lack in herself that only she recognized? "You know I've been married."

"Joshua has made me understand. He says that you were married to a Mormon, and he also said those marriages aren't legal. None of the territories or states recognize them except Utah. Fact, he said in a lot of places they crack down pretty hard on the guy caught living in plural marriage. Jail and such."

"Matthew—" She was feeling the pressure. "You deserve better than me, than this kind of marriage."

In his stillness she felt his awareness. Although it was dark now, she wondered if he were seeing into her thoughts as he spoke slowly, "I understand. Have you forgotten that I was married too? I don't expect it to be like it was with Amy. Josh says there's just no way to recapture the past. I guess I know what I'm asking. It's just that we have the chance to help each other and share life together." His voice was flat now. "We both need a partner."

Finally she promised to consider his proposal. They linked hands as they walked back up the path in the darkness, but Solali's heart was heavy. Before they parted she dared bring out one more problem. "You said something about making peace with your God. I still struggle with your God."

Rebecca was asleep when Solali entered their bedroom. She tiptoed across the room in the dark and leaned against the cool window. The moon was rising now, the kind of moon that spoke much to her people. It warned of the seasons to come. Its gentle brightness urged them to hurry on to new harvest fields. Soon it would be time for the gathering of nuts from the pine trees.

She closed her eyes and felt the life of her people possessing her, filling her with yearning. And there was Eagle. The cold, the days of hunger no longer worried her. But, she admitted as she leaned against the window frame, if there were no Eagle, then life with Matthew would be possible. It might even seem the best way. She watched the moon progress across the sky.

It was late and she moved restlessly. Fearful of disturbing Rebecca, she moved slowly across the room. Now at the door she paused, looking toward the quiet form of her friend. Thinking of the times in the past when Rebecca had awakened during the night, weeping and tearing at her pillow, she hesitated, holding her breath. When she had satisfied herself, listening to the deep, regular breathing, she slipped through the door.

From the head of the stairs, she saw a tiny fire glowing on the hearth. Joshua's bright head was bent over a book and after a second, she slipped down the stairs.

He looked up. The expectancy on his face disappeared as she moved into the light. "Hello, Solali. You can't sleep either?"

She shook her head and sat down opposite him. "The Bible?"

He nodded. "Don't like carrying the Book up the valley. It could get wet, and then where'd I be?"

"Rebecca has one." A shadow crossed his face and she added, "But I'm thinking you need the words very much."

He was staring into the fire and he replied soberly, "I'm beginning to think I need them more than anything else in my life." Glancing up he said, "But how about you? Rebecca's told me about the struggles she had trying to make you understand the difference between how you were taught concerning the Mormon god and about the true God."

Solali nodded and admitted, "Seems to only confuse. What I've learned keeps getting mixed up."

"Maybe you'd do well to read it for yourself."

"I have been—but I don't read well."

"You speak English very well, and you could learn to read better."

He moved to sit on the settle beside her. Placing the open Bible on her lap, he said, "I'll explain to you just what you can expect to find in the different parts. You get Rebecca to help you read. Any time you want you can use my Bible, just be careful with it."

Solali bent over the Book and her fingers pointed out the words just as Mrs. Tomkins at the school had taught her. Joshua gently moved her fingers down the page. She read, " 'For God so loved—' " She looked up. "That's what Rebecca says. She says that's the difference between the two Gods. I don't know what she means about obeying. How can you obey a god.? She says that we're to not be fearing this God. I don't understand how you can follow just love."

"Love must pull more strongly than fear." As Solali listened to Joshua, she was remembering the way Cynthia had shaken her head over Joshua's many trips into Utah Territory searching for Rebecca. Cynthia didn't understand love, either.

Solali turned her head to study the strong features of the man bending over the Book. She looked at the golden glow of his hair and skin. "Children of light. You really do belong together." A feeling tinged with envy touched her. "You do love Rebecca, don't you? It isn't because you are almost her brother, but it is more. It didn't take those newspapers and their fearful tales to make you go after her, did it?"

A muscle in Joshua's face twitched. For a second he looked at Solali, allowing her to see his eyes as they darkened, tortured into an expression very near the way Eagle had looked. Slowly she said, "I don't think I know what love is, either."

"Love," he said thoughtfully, as if wondering himself, "is it like a quiet river, bending and slowly changing? Or is it the cataracts crashing down with power, life—" he stopped.

Quickly he took up the Book and began to turn the pages. Now his hands were still. "I—I don't know where to turn. Solali, it nearly takes a lifetime of reading before you catch it all. Seems like it did with me."

"All of what?"

"The picture of God's love and patience with mankind. How He provided a way to rescue His people even when they didn't know they needed to be rescued. Reconciling—it's in there. It means to bring back to Him. All this is in there, but you'll have to read it for yourself."

"Joshua," she whispered, "I need something now. Isn't it possible? How do I compact a lifetime of reading to help me now?"

Joshua dropped to his knees beside Solali. Still holding the Book he studied her face. Neither of them heard the whisper of footsteps on the stairs. Footsteps that started, hesitated, then retreated. Joshua was speaking softly. "Solali, I do believe you really are wanting—do you believe the story about Jesus?"

"That he was God come to live here and to die?" She nodded.

"You know," he said, studying her with those intense blue eyes. "Solali, you know all the thinking about it isn't going to do you any good. Christianity is an invitation from God to you. You have to take up His offer. Do you really want to make this Jesus Christ your Savior forever? Remember, He's God. If you're saying that you want to belong to Him, remember, that means you'll be making Him the most important part of your life. You'll be giving Him the right to do anything He wants with your life. I doubt you understand what that means."

Her eyes were wide with excitement. "Joshua, I'm only full of yearning. I feel like Cynthia's little chicks trying to burst my shell."

"I think you must pray. Shall I say the words for you to repeat?"

She nodded and they bent their heads together. "I believe the Holy Lord Jesus Christ came to this earth and died for me. I accept that atonement, Lord Jesus. Because of Your love, because You died, I ask You to forgive my sins and allow me to become Your child. I want to live my life for You. I want You to be my God." Her words were breathy echoes of his. Now she blinked and smiled up at him.

"Look, there's something I want to read to you. And it's yours forever." He opened the Bible and found the place. " 'He came unto his own, and his own received him not. But as many as received him, to them gave he power to become the sons of God, *even* to them that believe on his name.' "

In the half-light of dawn Rebecca slipped from the bed, dressed and crept down the stairs. Taking Cynthia's old shawl from behind the kitchen door she wrapped it about her shoulders and slipped through the door.

The late summer dew was heavy on the grass and Rebecca's dress wiped a furrow through the meadow as she wandered. She knew the hem of her dress was becoming heavy with mois-

ture, but she tightened the shawl around her arms and continued to walk.

At the edge of the trees where Joshua cut firewood, she hesitated and looked down the valley toward the house. In sleep-
lessness, with her mind churning beyond rational thought, she
had felt the house pressing in upon her. Now alien, foe, not
friend. But this morning it was simply there, unmoving, un-
threatening. It wasn't the house pressing in upon her last night,
but the people it held. How deeply she was aware of those people
with their emotions, hidden thoughts, even fears; was there no
escape?

She studied the place and fought to calm her rage. If only
those people would leave her alone! Where was quietness and
peace to be found? There was no real peace. She had to accept
it. That scene last night—she must accept it too. But she could
not deny the jealousy, the surging anger she had felt last night,
when by the glow of the fire she had seen Solali and Joshua
with their heads together.

"Oh, my God!" she cried. The dew cascaded off the tips of
the fir branches splattering her face, but even the wetness didn't
cool her anger. Rebecca turned bitterly from the sight of the
house. "It's happening again. 'Tis the same old sick feelings,
the same betrayal. God, do You have no man on this earth who
will be true to one woman? Is that what I get for trusting a
man?" There was no answer, only the heaviness of her own
heart.

She tightened the shawl around her and plunged into the
trees, wanting only to be hidden from the view of the farm
nestled peacefully below.

She followed the trail cut by Joshua's wagon to the clearing,
still full of the bruised fragrance of freshly cut wood. She chose
a stump. Now shivering, she pulled her feet under her and
prepared to wait for the dawn and for the sound of the wagon
and team going down that road, carrying Joshua, Matthew, and
Mr. Smyth away from the farm.

Cynthia was preparing breakfast when Joshua and Matthew came into the kitchen. Eager to share the news with Re-

becca, Joshua looked around the room. "Where's Becky?" Cynthia shrugged and continued slicing bread. Solali came into the room and her eyes met Joshua's. He saw they were still filled with wonder. Impatiently he asked, "When's Becky coming? I want her to be the first to know."

"Oh," Solali blinked and looked around. "Isn't she here?"

Now Cynthia paused and waved the knife. "I 'spect she's gone out somewhere; my shawl's missing." The coffeepot began to boil over and Joshua snatched it up.

Matthew said, "I'm guessin' she's gone for a walk. There's a trace through the field and heading up to the trees."

"I'm not wanting to head for Pa's until I speak to her," Joshua said. He carefully set the coffeepot on the back of the stove and continued, "You have your breakfast and I'll go fetch her."

Rebecca was still sitting on the stump when the sun began to touch the trees with light. She stayed motionless when she heard the twig snap, waiting until the sun brightened his hair before she acknowledged his presence. Her voice was flat. "I expected you to be on your way by now."

"That means you've planned to avoid me?"

"I didn't sleep too well, needed the fresh air. Besides, I didn't think I'd be missed."

"And I'm to go without a hot breakfast."

"Cynthia's there. And Solali."

His eyes brightened, "Then you know about Solali? Did she tell you all that happened last night?"

Brushing off his question, not wanting to admit her ignorance, she jumped to her feet and tried to distract the ache in her heart with chatter. "Seems a waste, this gallivanting off all the time."

"Well, come along, I'll get my job done and be back here. Didn't know you were missing me so."

She tossed her head. "Oh, that's smart talk. Bet you're having a girl in every valley."

"Oh, yes, and I'm shinglin' and courtin' at the same time," he retorted. "Come along; breakfast will be ruined."

"Just think of the time you'd have saved in the running back and forth if you'd only snugged your houses right up together."

"There's an unclaimed section stuck between our places."

"I heard tell about the Donation Land Act. You're lucky the Mormons didn't hear about that. A Mormon and his passel of wives could take over the whole valley."

"Rebecca, what's got into you?"

"Nothing. But I see I'm going to need to teach Solali a few things. She's sure not much of a cook."

"Well, I know that. Now come along or Ma'll be throwing our breakfast to the chickens."

At a loss for words in the face of his amused calm, silently Rebecca hurried after him.

They were all around the table and the warm room was full of the delicious odor of coffee and bacon and eggs. As Rebecca slowly hung the shawl behind the door, she saw the pleased grin on Joshua's face as he waited beside her chair. When she sat down, he moved behind Solali's chair.

"Now we're all here together, I want to be the one to tell you," he began in his pleased voice. Rebecca saw him touch Solali lightly on the shoulder. Catching her breath, Becky ducked her head and waited. She fought the childish urge to stuff her fingers in her ears. He was speaking again. "This is something wonderful, and I want to tell you all about it." Again he paused and Rebecca looked at Solali, seeing her suddenly shy. "Last night," Joshua said, "Solali became a believer, a child of God."

Rebecca gasped, Matthew's face brightened, and Cynthia passed the eggs. Matthew peered around his mother's arm. "I'm wishin' it could have been me to lead her in the way. But I don't have the easy tongue." He was beaming shyly, possessively.

With a sigh, Rebecca picked up her fork. Her hand was trembling and she pressed the fork against the plate. "Here, have an egg." Joshua shoved the platter at her. She passed the platter and stared at her plate, but she was seeing that nighttime scene from the head of the stairs.

Joshua was finishing his breakfast, draining the last of his coffee. He was looking at her and the questions were still there. "Becky?"

"I—" The fork was moving faster, but she contemplated the

lump in her throat and decided it would be best to just mash the egg on the plate.

"Rebecca, I would like a word with you." The row of eyes fastened first on Rebecca, then moved to Joshua.

"Well, I 'spect you'd better speak up so's we'll all hear," Matthew drawled, "Unless you want Ma to weed the garden at six in the morning and me to head down the road and Solali here—"

"Might be a good idea at that," Joshua interrupted. "On the other hand, might be we'll go weed the patch, since Rebecca's already soaked."

"Joshua—" helplessly Rebecca began, then fell silent. His hand was on the back of her chair.

"Oh, pawsh, go in the parlor," Cynthia snorted. "You think a body's all ears? Solali, go fetch Kalli for breakfast." Solali's face brightened and a smile spread across her face as she left the room.

Matthew was in the wagon, waiting at the front door. He flicked the reins along the backs of the team and settled lower on the seat and tilted his hat over his eyes. Rebecca stared through the window at him, ignoring Joshua.

His hand on her shoulder brought her around, gently but firmly. He was shaking his head. "I don't think I'll ever on this earth understand women. I'm getting the idea that everyone's in on a big secret except me. Becky," he paused and shifted from one foot to the other while a perplexed frown creased his forehead. "You tried to slip out without saying good-bye. Why?"

She shook her head. "Rebecca Wolstone, I'm waiting." She jerked her head up to meet his eyes. Wolstone, not Jacobson—and she could see he meant it. He wasn't thinking of the past or anything else. Her hand slipped toward her throat and he reached for it.

"Why do you look like that? Are you fearing me? You know I said I wouldn't pressure you." He hesitated while he continued to study her face; then slowly he reached for her. Trembling, Rebecca came, conscious of him with all her mind and body.

His arm held her close as his left hand lifted her chin. She was filled with the glory of him, the light in his eyes and the smile behind his golden beard. "Children of light," she murmured Solali's words. Slowly his arm tightened, bringing her closer, measuring her response. She closed her eyes, suddenly weighted, shy. In the moment he held her close before touching her lips, she felt the gold ring pressing against her face.

"My Becky," he whispered. "Always and forever you've been mine, but do you realize, through all these years I've never held you like this, and I've never kissed you?" Now Rebecca opened her eyes. With her two hands she wiped away the tears from her eyes before she wrapped her arms around his neck.

CHAPTER 14

In the days that followed it seemed to Rebecca that she was wrapped with the essence of Joshua. And while she ached with loneliness, his touch and his presence informed her that she would never again be unloved.

But even in the lonely hours she found that life must go on. There was work to do. Tasks waited.

It was Rebecca's secret; the very air was golden because of him. At least she thought it her secret. Finally Cynthia rescued the half-pared apples, the pan and knife.

Turning to Solali she demanded, "Find her something to do that takes only a half a mind. Where the rest of hers has fled, I don't know. But I do believe we'll need to be having a weddin' before Pa and I can move up to the house."

Rebecca moved. "Wedding? Oh—but that's—well, maybe."

She tried to separate herself from the dream, but she continued to hang suspended, useless, knowing only the counting of time until he would return. Beyond Cynthia's ever-questioning look was Solali's wistful expression. Rebecca tried to reason with herself, tried to grasp reality and found it only added substance to her dreams.

On the day Joshua was to return, Matthew came alone. "Pa's hurt," he reported. "Nothing too serious. He slipped from the roof and wrenched his back. Joshua made him go to bed and stay there and he's sent me to fetch Ma. We've got things pretty cozy right now. I can go back and stay until he's feeling better, then—" He paused to study Solali's face before adding, "I'm of a mind to move back down to Salem before the rain starts. We've had a pack of trouble with squatters anyway."

Rebecca saw the exchange of glances between Solali and Matthew. Now she picked up the word. "Squatters—what's that?"

"Them who walk in and take over. If they're let to stay long enough, it's nigh on to impossible to prove you've had honest intentions toward the land in the first place."

Matthew moved restlessly around the kitchen and Cynthia got to her feet. "I 'spect we might as well get that wagon loaded and head out. Don't like to be caught on the road after dark. Mortons tell that the Indians have been causing problems down by Jackson Creek. The thieving bunch, they want the grub without working for it."

Rebecca saw Solali wince. She hesitated, wondering what she could say to remove the sting of the woman's words. But after a moment Becky shrugged and, turning to Cynthia, said, "I'll help you gather up the things you want to take this trip. Do you want Matt to load in the little chest too?" She saw that Cynthia was still muttering as she went up the stairs.

"Becky, don't," Solali said softly. "It doesn't matter." She gave her a push toward the stairs.

Rebecca went to carry down a bundle of quilts. When she passed the kitchen door with her load, she saw Matthew and Solali facing each other across the table.

Settling her bundle beside the front door, Rebecca turned just as Solali spoke. Her voice was low, meant only for Matthew, but the earnestness of her tone had Rebecca's attention. "You see, Matthew, much as I like you and respect you, much as I want to raise your little Thomas, I can't marry you."

On her way upstairs, Rebecca was opposite the kitchen door, seeing Solali with her head bowed. Her softly spoken words were indistinct, but Rebecca heard, "Not fair—it's wrong. Eagle has my heart."

"But Eagle has left," Matthew said and then waited. Suddenly realizing that she was eavesdropping, Rebecca ran up the stairs. Behind her came Matthew's heavy voice saying, "If you change your mind, ever, Solali, I'll be waiting."

Solali, Rebecca, and Kalli watched the wagon rumble down the lane. The loneliness and the regret pressed in upon Rebecca and she wondered what the two Indian women were feeling. Kalli's wide eyes studied Solali as she turned toward the kitchen.

That evening, after Rebecca and Solali had milked the cows and fed the chickens and pigs, they closed the house against the evening chill and nighttime sounds.

Although it was only dusk, Solali put the lamp in the middle of the kitchen table. With no men to cook for and with Cynthia's hearty appetite gone, they scrambled eggs and browned bread on the hospitable warmth of the stove.

Kalli was a small chunk of silence at the end of the table as she fed the child. Solali still persisted in her attempts to teach Kalli English. "Bread," she held up the slice; now, pointing to the stove, she said, "Toast."

Kalli's face was blank. Solali shrugged and reached for the butter. After she had spread the toast with the butter, she handed it to the little boy. "Baby," said Kalli beaming.

Rebecca sat down across the table from Solali and handed the eggs to Kalli. "One thing," she said, "we'll not have to worry about Cynthia hearing our conversation secondhand."

"How long will you keep your silence with her?" Solali asked. "I see the questions big in her eyes. It's not good." She was shaking her head as she ladled jam onto her plate.

Rebecca sighed, "It makes a strain. I feel it constantly and I see the questions too. Whatever Joshua said to her to make her keep her silence must have been strong. She's always been prone to speak her mind." She raised her hands helplessly. "But what am I to do? Solali—I am so fearful. You saw how she was with the newspapers."

Solali picked at her eggs, and Rebecca was conscious of her brooding expression as she looked at her. Finally she placed her fork on the table and leaned forward. "Solali, I'm feeling *your* questions too. I have for weeks now. We've no vow of silence."

She nodded, "True, except the vows our minds hold."

"What do you mean?"

"Rebecca, I'm fearful for you. Since that—all this time since it happened. That, back there at the Meadows." Her words were choppy and her eyes were begging for Rebecca's understanding.

She took a deep breath and started again. "Please. You have been frozen away from the feelings. I must speak. My people weep and talk. You have done neither. There's just been those terrible dreams at night and then you push them away. I thought time would heal but as it has passed, I've seen you become hard like the lake in January. Is that good? Will it ever cease to be, just by your pretending? Is this really the way of the white man? I hear them say to stiffen your back and don't complain. I heard that much while I was a Mormon. Is that all your God can do for you? I wonder, because I cannot see any good in this way. Like a wound hidden, there is no healing."

"I am not certain I understand you." Rebecca was breaking her toast into neat little squares which she then carefully spread with apple jelly.

"Then look at me; you are using the toast to hide away again."

Rebecca looked and was surprised at the hint of mockery in her voice as she said, "I'm looking and I see a young Indian maiden telling an older woman how to face life."

For an instant Solali's face became closed and then she said softly, "Can you not let your heart be open? Joshua has been teaching me about Jesus and I have been reading the Book. Please, Rebecca, I am trying to understand too. And I see this way you live as a—" She hesitated for a long moment while her brow furrowed in frustration. Finally she straightened and held out her hands with forefingers extended. "See, like this." Slowly she crossed the fingers at right angles.

When Solali dropped her hands, her face was troubled. "I must understand how to believe and trust in this Jesus, since He is my God. The Book shows that while Jesus lived among men, He was touching them, loving them, and healing them. Joshua says He is alive, in heaven praying for us before the Father."

She hesitated again and then softly said, "When I look at you, I don't see Him alive. I don't see Him touching you and healing you." The silence in the room grew and the darkness settled.

When the silence was impossible to bear, Kalli stood up and began carefully stacking the dishes. Now that she had their attention, she smiled with satisfaction and marched to the nail on the wall which held the dishpan. Dropping a chunk of brown soap into the pan, she reached for the teakettle and poured a stream of hot water on the soap. She was smiling with delight at their attention. Carefully she stretched her hand toward the steaming dishpan.

"No, Kalli!" Rebecca jumped to her feet and ran for the dipper of cold water. With a gasp of relief, she poured and tested, "Now, Kalli, you wash."

She sat down and they watched Kalli add the dishes to the pan and pick up the dishcloth. Rebecca felt as if she had been stretched to the breaking point; now the tension was dissolving as completely as the soap melting in the pan.

She leaned her elbows on the table and tried to sort through the emotional jumble of her feelings. Solali's words had stripped bare something she had been hiding—hiding so completely that she didn't know it existed. Solali was watching her.

"It's all right," she whispered. "Solali, I'm sorry I snapped. It's just—well, please say no more now."

And the next day, while the sun was bright and Kalli was busy with the dishpan again, Solali held Thomas and brought out the words once again.

She said, "I've read the story of Jesus and that woman at the well. You know, the one who had been living with a man who wasn't her husband. It was like Jesus had been reading my thoughts and suddenly He was saying: 'I know what you are wondering, Solali; I say go and sin no more.' "

"And what *were* you thinking?" Rebecca whispered.

"I was feeling the belonging to Jesus Christ, and knowing that I must be holy. Then I wondered about my past—the years I lived as a plural wife and my rebellion and running away from it all. I guess everything was making me feel like a sinful woman."

"Is that why you told Matthew you wouldn't marry him?"

Solali waited for a moment before she answered, "No. Seeing you with Joshua changed everything for me. But that was only the end of it. It was Joshua who helped me see the beginning, and that started to change my thinking. First, I was thinking that your God would want me to marry a white man, just like the Mormons required me to marry a man with two other wives. But that was all wrong. Joshua showed me in the Bible that Jesus Christ is the atonement for sins for *everyone*. He died to give me all that I was trying to earn for myself by being a good person and doing what I was told to do."

"Yes, I know all that."

"I understand now, it's a gift, this salvation. Joshua called it being reconciled to God, being able to call Him Father just like Jesus did. Joshua said I didn't have to do anything to deserve it. I just had to take it. When I knelt down and told Jesus Christ I was sorry for my sins and that I wanted to have His atonement, then I knew I didn't have to marry Matthew to be a Christian. But later, I was thinking about how things are going. Those things Cynthia said about Jackson Creek."

Rebecca leaned across the table. "Solali, you're thinking about how the white man has pushed the Indians off their land. How they've made promises and then haven't kept them. You know I am ashamed of all this."

"But they will continue to do it. We are weak people. Soon we won't exist. I can see how I would have a better life by marrying a white man. Remember, I know what it's like to go to school and live in a warm house in the winter and dig a garden patch instead of living in a willow hut and following the harvest of nature. At one time it was a good life. Now the white people are making it very hard for us to live as our fathers lived. I chose to escape. I would marry Matthew."

"But you've told him no. Why?"

She lifted her head and her dark eyes were dreamy. "I saw you and Joshua. I understand that you belong together and that there is a great love."

Rebecca took an unsteady breath and whispered, "Yes, there is. I'm almost afraid to think about it. Seems like a wind will blow it away."

Solali was studying her face and Rebecca pressed her hands against her warm cheeks. Solali said, "You look as if you aren't quite awake, as if you are afraid to face the dawn." She was silent now, and a dark shadow seemed to move across her face.

"Don't look like that. I'll pray you and Eagle will have the same love."

She was shaking her head. "I wasn't thinking about that. It's you. Rebecca, how can you be happy when you haven't cried?"

"Solali!" Rebecca jumped to her feet. "You're digging at me. You don't understand white people. We don't believe in letting out all the dark thoughts."

Solali rested her hands on the tabletop and leaned toward Rebecca. Her eyes demanded Rebecca's attention. "And you will go through life pretending those things didn't really happen? Rebecca, I heard your screams while the fever gripped you. You relived that night over and over. I heard you cry, 'Please, don't kill the children!' And then you cried, 'Timmy, Timmy!' Who was Timmy? And when your baby was born—do you remember what you said?"

Rebecca's hands clasped her throat. "Solali," she whispered, "you'll kill me, don't . . ."

"Rebecca, I know enough about Jesus—"

"Solali!" she screamed and the sound tore through the kitchen. Now whirling and pressing her hands to her ears, she ran from the room, crying, "Don't ever say it again. Now leave me alone!" She ran across the parlor and into the room shared by Matthew and Joshua.

Dimly she remembered that when her sobbing ceased, Solali crept into the room and pulled the quilt over her shoulders.

When Joshua came, it was Solali who met him as he led his horse to the corral. His smile faded when he saw her haggard face. "It's Rebecca," she said with a weary sigh. "Please stay here and let me tell you about it before you see her. I am to be blamed for it all, and it is much worse than I thought. I knew she must mourn, but I didn't understand the—the darkness of it all."

Slowly Joshua pitched hay to his horse and then picked up

a towel. As Solali continued to bring out the painful words, he rubbed down the sweating horse.

"You've ridden her hard," Solali paused to reflect.

"Yes, I was anxious to see Becky." He faced Solali. "Your words aren't making too much sense. A dream, a nightmare? Becky is a healthy, normal woman. She'll get over it."

"You'll have to see," Solali whispered. "Joshua, I didn't understand. I thought only that she needed to cry over that baby before she could come alive again."

Joshua frowned. "I think I'm beginning to see. You're saying you see things I don't. That her quietness and then her laughter was telling you her problem. Yes, I've seen it's from one to the other she has moved. Now I'm seeing more. There's a fence about her heart. I was ready to accept that as the grown-up Becky, but you're saying it shows her hurt." He paced back and forth in the barn as Solali talked on.

"I listened to her during the bad time when she first came to our village. There was fear and anger in her. I saw the wild expression in her eyes and heard the screams. I don't know how she can hold it in. Sometimes during the night hours, it haunts me." Solali caught up with Joshua and looked into his face. "Does Jesus still heal?"

Joshua stopped and stared at her. Slowly he said, "Solali, Jesus Christ is alive. The Bible says He's the same, and He did it then. I remember a verse that goes like this: 'Who his own self bare our sins in his own body on the tree, that we, being dead to sins, should live unto righteousness: by whose stripes ye were healed.'"

Now he sighed with relief and smiled down at Solali. "It isn't hopeless. We have a kind heavenly Father who has given us all things in Jesus Christ. Solali, we must pray for Rebecca."

As he walked rapidly toward the house, Solali ran to keep up with him, crying, "But you don't understand—"

"But I believe." As he reached for the door, he patted her shoulder. "I've the faith to believe that Jesus Christ can handle Rebecca's problems. He has so far."

He found her at the stove. Without looking up she continued to slice potatoes into the frying pan. When she finished, she turned her head and he saw her eyes were shadowed, remote. "Joshua, you're back. How nice." He leaned to kiss her and she moved away. "How's your pa? Is it serious?"

"Naw, a stiff back for a couple of days. He's still tough. He and Ma'll be back down here next week. Then, they're saying, if there's any visitin' to be done, we'll have to come see them."

"Why are they coming back?" He knew Rebecca was making conversation.

"Pa's going to take Ma into Salem and they're going to have a shoppin' spree before the rains begin. We got a good price for the wheat and the money's burnin' a hole in Pa's pocket."

"Just like always." Rebecca's voice was sharp.

"Just like always," Joshua echoed, more caught by the sharpness in Rebecca's voice than he was by the memory of his father's past spending habits.

Kalli came into the kitchen carrying Matthew's baby. Her child ran to Joshua and lifted his arms.

"Hello, big guy." Joshua swung him high.

"Hello," the child mimicked, giggling as he nestled against Joshua's arm.

Clasping the child close, Joshua whispered, "Hey, I'd like to keep you forever. You're a good young'un." He addressed Solali. "Matt's serious about leaving for Salem. May go next week."

"Is he angry with me?" she answered.

"No, I think he understands. Matt was pretty wrapped up in his Amy."

"Eagle?"

He shook his head. "I haven't seen any more of him. He sure wasn't talkin' when he left here, so I don't know what—" Solali turned away with a sigh.

"Hey!" Joshua was watching Kalli with a pleased grin. She had given the baby to Solali and now she was busy carrying plates and forks to the table. She brought bread to the table and skillfully sliced it. "Lady, you're doing fine." Joshua reached awkwardly around his armload of child to pat Kalli's shoulder.

"Fine," the child echoed, swinging from Joshua's neck. "Fine," echoed again from Kalli, an uncharacteristic glitter of expression in her eye. Silently Rebecca brushed past carrying the platter of meat.

After supper Joshua took Rebecca's hand. "Let's leave Solali and Kalli with the clean-up. Seems that young lady is taking pride in what she's learning to do."

"Eagle seemed to think she would be content staying here forever," Solali said as she got to her feet. "Yes, Rebecca, go on. You need the fresh air." Addressing Joshua, she said, "She's scarcely been out of the house for a week now."

Rebecca hesitated and Joshua nudged her toward the door. With Kalli's child swooping around their heels, they headed through the autumn-bare fields. "Soon it's frost and scorch, that's the autumn weather here; then comes the rain." Joshua picked a stalk of dried grass to nibble. "Some say it looks dead then when it's picked clean. It just reminds me of the work that's been done. Week after next I aim to plow the wheat field and get ready for the winter rains to do my work, keepin' the little wheat seeds happy 'til summer."

Still she was silent. "Guess I'll cut us some more firewood tomorrow," he reflected, then, "Rebecca, after Matt collects his household and heads for home, how's about us and Solali going to Salem? You know it's the capital of the Territory. There's always something going on there. Right now things are moving swift toward our getting statehood. It'll be exciting for you. How about it?"

"Joshua." They had reached the corrals and she turned to back against the log fence. He watched her take a deep breath and then she said, "I can't marry you. I'm sorry. It just won't work."

He stepped close and bent down to look into her eyes. "Seems to me you've changed your mind awful fast. Mind tellin' me why?"

She moved her head wearily. "I've a heart to try my hand at school teaching."

"That's strange. First time I've heard you mention it since we've come home."

"Joshua, leave me be. You said you wouldn't pressure me and I'm holding you to that."

"Mind kissin' me and then telling me that again?"

"No." He saw she was breathless and he pressed again.

"Solali's said you've had a rough time of it while I was gone. Rebecca, I know what I'm getting. It's you I want and I'm willing to handle the problems. Let's forget about the past and just work at building a life together. I need you as much—maybe more'n you need me."

She stood tall and ramrod stiff. "I'm not making myself understood. Joshua, I *can't* marry you."

"You're not married." Her eyes were darkening and he pushed the brutal words at her. "You've lived with a man. You've been misused and tortured. I take it you can't face the risk of it happening again. Becky, I can't tell you I'll never disappoint you; but *hurt you* deliberately? That won't happen. If you're fearin' me, then that's something I can't control. You've seen me for what I am. I'm not pretending and you know that. From the outside of me clear through to the heart, you see me as I am. If that isn't good enough, well say so and I'll not bother you again."

"Oh, Joshua," her voice broke. "It isn't that. You're beautiful all the way through, and you're deserving of so much better."

"After spending years hunting for you, are you trying to tell me I don't know my own mind?"

She was shaking her head. "Don't pressure me. I've made my decision and there'll be no changing it now."

He stepped close to her and clasped her forearms in his warm hands. "Don't you think you owe a body enough to come clean and say the real reason?"

For a moment she was motionless, her head cocked as if listening and then she moved. Jerking herself free, she turned and ran to the house.

Joshua followed slowly, knowing suddenly how futile, even powerless his efforts were. His shoulders sagged and then straightened. In the past, in the black days, he had known only the burden and the prayers.

CHAPTER 15

Behind the house, under the low eaves, the stack of firewood was growing. Matthew came and left, taking with him his son and Kalli with her child. He would find someone else to live with them to keep the tongues from wagging. The oak and apple trees held a hint of autumn color.

Again Rebecca refused to go to Salem, but the pain in her eyes when Joshua asked was enough to give him heart.

He was waiting patiently and he knew that Rebecca was aware of it. While he bided his time, he was seeing Rebecca grow thin and pale.

One night Joshua awakened to a whisper of sound from the parlor. As he lay in the darkness, he recognized the familiar sound, one that had penetrated his sleep often during the past days. Knowing now what he would find, he dressed and quietly crossed the darkened house. In the shelter of the high-backed settle, Rebecca crouched, shivering.

One glance confirmed his guesses: the dreams Solali had talked about. In her white, tear-stained face and shivering form, lighted only by the dying embers of the fire, he saw her undisguised despair.

Going back to his room he took the quilt from the bed and brought it to Rebecca. She allowed him to wrap her in it and tuck it about her feet. He poked at the fire and added wood before he sat down on the stool.

"Don't say it." Her voice was thick and weary. "It's simply that I can't sleep and I didn't want to disturb Solali."

"Forget the—all else." His voice was rough. "I only want to help you now and I can't do that until you'll allow it."

"Just dreams." She shivered and pulled the quilt close. "By morning I forget."

"Tell me about them." Her stony face gave him his answer. "Would you like tea?" She shook her head. He kept the silence, wondering what to do when words failed.

Finally she stirred. "Joshua, leave me to sort things out. Before, when I kissed you, I honestly didn't realize—" More silence and then she continued with a controlled sob. "There's such ugliness inside. I thought I was whole, mending. I'm thinking God's telling me how unfit I am to even dream of a—of life again."

He poked at the wood and waited, constrained in a way he couldn't understand.

Out of a long silence she spoke, almost dreamily, and her words chilled him. "I know that Jesus Christ has redeemed me for all eternity through His precious blood—" For a moment there were ragged sobs, revealing an anguish he hadn't guessed. "But I can't bear the burden of the past. Why will He not release me now to go to Him? It would have been better—my baby. Why must I live on in the torture of the past? I yearn so for release."

It was much later when he said wearily, "Becky." He was fingering the gold ring strung on rawhide about his neck. "If I hadn't gone to California, if I'd come straight to Utah, then this—" He dropped the ring and looked up at her. "I guess I'm sayin' it's just as much my fault as yours."

The fire died, winking out in its final glow. Now the kitchen window lightened and the rooster crowed. When Joshua got to his feet, still wordless, Rebecca's face was only a pale shadow. His hands hung helplessly by his side as he walked back to his bedroom.

And the next night, when she would have followed Solali up the stairs, he stopped her. "I've been thinking, Rebecca. Come listen."

"Joshua, no, please."

His voice was ragged with weariness, cutting in on her protest. "You're thinking God has brought you this far and that now He will abandon you. Don't you think He is your *Father*, that He wants you to have happiness and the fulfillment of all that a woman holds dear?"

She moved restlessly and he forced his words quickly, trying to prevent her retreat. "I don't see God as being like that. Is it possible that the years of teaching by that other church has left fragments in your thoughts that aren't thoughts from God?"

"I don't understand."

"You make me think of something the Apostle Paul wrote— it went like this. He said, 'You foolish Galatians, are you bewitched? You started with the Spirit; are you trying to do it all on your own now?'"

"Say it, Joshua."

"You're giving up on following Jesus Christ. You started just the way you were supposed to start, but now you're handling the reins. Just like a young filly throwing herself into the race and forgetting who's the rider."

"No, you've got it all wrong. I'm knowing I'll never be fit to be a wife and mother. I accept this as being from God."

"Why are you talking like this?"

"It's before me, the facts. I know how I am inside."

"If you're saying you're afraid you'll never bear another child, Rebecca, that's not why I'm wanting you. I love you for yourself. If there's never a child, it won't change how I feel about you."

She burst away from him, away from the tenderness in his voice and said impatiently. "You don't understand."

"Yes, I do. I understand that you've problems you won't air to me." She was shaking her head and desperately he said, "Solali told me about all she lived through with you when you were so badly wounded and ill with the fever. And then she told me how it was when the baby was born. Rebecca, other women live through these bad times and recover to live normal lives."

"I know!" She was shouting while the tears streamed down her face. "I've been treated to their stories since I've been here. I'm not saying I've had it worse."

He held out his arms, "My little Becky. Don't you see that

I love you? How I wish you'd let me share the load with you."

She avoided his arms, "No, you don't." She paused and wiped at the tears. Now wearily she added, "And you'll force it from me, won't you? Joshua, I'd soil you with my ugliness." In a moment her tears were dried and her eyes were flashing. She drew herself up and her face contorted with rage. Leaning close to him, she hissed, "You would never carry this load. You see, *I hate that man on the Meadow.* I've lived a long time with the burden, but now I see he didn't have the right to take my life from me because I disobeyed him. There was no divine redemption in killing me. That man is not my god and never has been. No longer do I accept Brigham Young as ruler of my life and eternity. Not one thing he says can send me to hell, but together those two men stripped me of the only thing I had left in this world—my baby.

"Don't look so shocked, Joshua. You don't think I can hate like this because I lost a child? How can you judge what a baby can mean until you've desperately wanted a child and then to have cuddled him in your body those long months, only to have him denied life and stripped from you?"

"Rebecca—" Joshua's voice pleaded.

"Those men did it. Andrew, because he was obeying counsel; and Brigham Young, because he raised himself up as god and dictated with the power of life and death. He chose death for me." She paused only briefly and then lashed out again.

"And don't tell me I'm to forgive if I will be forgiven. I'm not forgetting that I was in all those difficulties because I was minding a God who knew and cared. He could have at least allowed me to have my baby. The rest I believe I could learn to live with, but this I cannot."

Joshua's eyes sought hers, but she looked away and pushed his hands from her.

"Yes, you might say I tried to bargain with God. I obey if He gives me my baby. Even on that hot ride across the desert when I tried to save those people's lives, I was expecting God to treat me like I was something special."

"And you're complaining," Joshua said slowly, "because God didn't act in the manner you chose for Him to act?"

Slowly he turned and sat down on the stool in front of the fire. For a long time he gazed into the glowing coals, watching them change from fire and warmth to a feeble glow and then dull ash. The things that he thought he would never admit surfaced in his thoughts, and they roamed through his mind, troubling him.

It was one thing to pray and feel sweet release, but it was quite another to pray and feel increased agony, especially when that agony must remain faceless, unnamed.

He was still pondering the significance of the words the Lord had burned into his thoughts when his only reason for living had been to find Rebecca. And, thinking back to those days, he found himself finally admitting his dark moment.

It was his groping, trusting, blind instincts which had led him on that final trip into Utah Territory. But even in the worst of times, he had felt a sureness, a sense of direction, moving through him. Until that last day.

Once again he felt the total desolation of that moment when he had been informed of Rebecca's death. There on that wind-battered mountain, confronted by the nameless stranger with the cold eyes, dealt that message, Joshua's faith shattered.

For hours as he wandered, his God was dead. Even at this minute Joshua's heart was wrenching as he remembered his moment of abandoned faith.

With a sigh he straightened and turned to Rebecca. "I guess it isn't in us to ever know God so completely that we don't sometimes stagger under the load. Rebecca, you're thinking my faith's always been nigh perfect. It isn't.

"If Eagle hadn't rescued me out of that snowstorm and brought me to you, I'd a plum walked off the edge of the earth without an upward glance. And all that, heaped upon the encouraging things the Spirit had been saying to me for months."

He saw a spark of interest on her face. "The Spirit," she whispered leaning forward. "What did He say?"

"You need to understand how I was feeling. I was plain tuckered out with praying and hoping and trying to understand the load He was putting on me to keep looking for you. I'd been at it for years, and I couldn't understand it. The thought kept comin' through to me that He was trying to offer you a chance to escape. I didn't know what you must escape, but I prayed the words. Then I hit the bottom. It seemed I couldn't say the words one more time. Seems then I was hearing Him say new words to me, and I was hearing them as a promise."

He gestured toward the dying fire. "I've never wanted to say them to you, mostly because I didn't like the thrust of them, and I wasn't sure of the reason why He must work this way when He had the power to rattle Utah Territory until you dropped out." He tried to grin but knew it was without humor. Rebecca's eyes were still dark in the pale oval of her face. She waited.

"It was the words God used through the prophet Amos."

"What were they?"

" '. . . and ye were as a firebrand plucked out of the burning.' "

She slowly backed into the corner of the settle and he could no longer see her eyes. After a long time he said, "Rebecca?" There was no answer, nothing more to be said.

Joshua got to his feet and began pacing the room, moving between the fireplace and the front windows. He was no longer restraining Rebecca, demanding an audience with her, but she continued to sit, watching him pace.

The fire had died, leaving the room in shadows. He stopped in front of her. "I honestly believe that if God through Jesus Christ is able to rescue us from the judgment fires, He is equally able to rescue us from ourselves. I keep seeing those lashes across His back. For every one of them, He's won our healing. And the healing isn't complete until it goes clear through to the mind. Body, soul, and mind, we belong to Him; we must."

Now Rebecca jumped to her feet and headed for the stairs. He was saying, "Ask, Rebecca."

She paused at the top of the stairs and said, "But you see, don't you? You see the hate that I am inside. I will not allow you to live your life with this burden."

"It isn't necessary. Ask, Rebecca."

The room was barely light with dawn when Solali slipped from the bed and left the room. Rebecca lay straining to understand every whisper of sound that came from below. Joshua would be leaving today for one last trip up the mountain to his pa's house. Would he insist on seeing her again before he left? Her heavy heart trembled away from contact with him.

The sky was pink when she heard a gentle nicker from his horse. Creeping to the window, she knelt with her elbows on the trunk. Joshua and Solali stood beside the horse for a moment more and then he mounted. Did his last glance toward the house search out her window? She shrank back.

When Rebecca finally dressed and went downstairs, Solali was busy in the kitchen. Rebecca's guilty conscience reminded her that if Joshua had told Solali about last night, it wasn't evident in her easy manner. She glanced up. "Sleepyhead. Joshua has left for his pa's section. Said to tell you good-bye."

Briefly there was curiosity in her eyes and Rebecca turned away. Solali reminded, "Today is the day the women get together at the Nortons' for sewing. Are we going?"

Rebecca nodded with a wry smile. She helped herself to the cracked wheat warming on the back of the stove. "I suppose so. There's not much else to do. I don't believe we can dry another batch of apples; there's too much moisture in the air."

" 'Tis true. It's not like the desert country. Even the clothes take forever to dry here."

CHAPTER 16

That afternoon Solali and Rebecca saddled horses and went into Waltstown. Solali remarked as they rode along, "Don't know that I want sitting all afternoon with a dab of needlework, but I like the ride." Then she added, "Besides, I want to see their houses. Seems the people aren't as poor about here as the Saints were."

"Solali," Rebecca said in a panic, "don't mention the Saints to these women."

"You know I won't. I'm hearkening to what you've said, though I know not why we should worry so. Seems a body would adjust to the idea we've left the church and now are following Jesus Christ."

"I'm still so fearful; I dare not let it slip out we were one of them."

"Is it fearful? I'm shunning their questions."

Rebecca didn't answer. There were those deeply buried thoughts burning in her. She tried to fasten her attention on the beauty around them. They crossed the McKenzie River as it slipped down through the little valley before slanting north to join the Willamette. Just before it entered Waltstown, it gentled and meandered quietly through the village.

The foliage along the road was touched with the colors of autumn and the annual grasses were drying. But the lush greenness of Oregon was still evident in the hemlock and fir as well as the meadow grass and the bushes and undergrowth along the river.

"Do you suppose this country will ever have the dead brown we had back there? At this time of year even the evergreens looked tired and dusty."

They had reached the outskirts of town and both women fell silent. The town clustered about one long main street. Down the length of the street were scattered the shops. There was a lawyer's office now, tucked in between the hat shop and the blacksmith's shop. The hardware store and the grocery shared a common roof and canopy. Across the way was the church, neat with white clapboard and a small, square belfry. As if in deference to its importance, the grounds of the church spread out like ample skirts, offering grass and shade to all.

Rebecca pointed. "If this were back east, they'd call it the town square. Here it's not quite big enough or square enough. It's just plain old folksy church grounds." She lowered her voice now as if afraid her thoughts would slip through. "What's different here is the planed board houses. Not a one adobe, and not too many log cabins here."

Solali chuckled. "Adobe, in this rainy country? You'd wake up some morning to find your house had melted away during the night. There you'd be in the middle of a mud puddle, in bed while the neighbors watched."

They passed the store, the blacksmith shop, and the school-house. "I think the Nortons' is that place with the blue shutters. Oh, my, aren't they pretty?"

The house was small and lined with women dressed in their best calico. Knitting needles flashed and the crotchet thread unrolled; while the fancy bits of stitchery were admired, the conversation shifted lightly about the room.

Rebecca looked around, trying to spot some of the women she had met at the last sewing bee. There was the tiny Mrs. Crocket. She smiled and nodded. Once again Rebecca searched the woman's face as she wondered about the stories she had been told of her experiences on the overland trip to Oregon.

After Rebecca and Solali had studied every detail of the parlor and the kitchen beyond, and then listened to the conversation, their eyes met with amusement. Solali, whispered,

"Adobe not withstanding, womenfolk are the same everywhere."

But there was Solali. While Betty Hanson talked about her layette and the new cradle her husband was making, Rebecca watched her friend. She was interested in the women, their dress, their homes, but there was a difference. Long before the tea and cake was served, Rebecca saw the faraway expression in her eyes. The stitches she poked in the pillow cover came slower, the thread tugged with indifference.

Later as they rode home, Rebecca said, "You didn't enjoy yourself?"

Solali looked startled. She waited until they had left Waltstown behind and then she said, "I guess I'm just now accepting it." She glanced quickly toward Rebecca. "This life just isn't the life for me."

Rebecca wanted to mention Eagle, but the unhappy droop to Solali's lips kept her silent.

Evening was well upon them before they turned down their own lane. The dark shadows filled Rebecca with uneasiness. As she and Solali took their milk pails and went to the barn, Rebecca reached out to touch Solali. "I'm glad more than I can say that you're here with me. It's a lonesome place after dark."

There was Solali's quick look and even in the twilight Rebecca saw the concern. Before she had finished milking her cows, the brooding shadows were back upon her spirit. She tried to brush them away as they walked to the house. "Seems a good time to start some cheese. We'll never use all this milk with Joshua gone."

Solali set her pail inside the house. "Mr. Evans at the store said he'd buy butter. Joshua ought to get more pigs to fatten." She turned away. "I'm going to pick some tomatoes."

Rebecca entered the house. The silence of the place swept about her and she was conscious of every sound. The wind brushed a branch against the kitchen window and wood in the box beside the stove slipped as Solali entered and slammed the door. When Solali stood just inside the door, caught in an attitude of listening, Rebecca knew she felt it too.

"Seems strange," Rebecca said slowly, "the place was burstin' with life one minute and now there's just the two of us." Solali's dark eyes were wary, waiting. Rebecca moved quickly, trying to shake off the mood. "We're a bunch of silly ones. What's there to be afraid of in Oregon?"

Solali didn't answer and after a moment Rebecca went to shove kindling into the stove. "Would you like a pancake for supper?" Solali nodded and went to sit at the table.

"Rebecca," she said slowly, "do you ever think about—well, about things that happened back there and wonder? About the beliefs of the church. Would those—those things reach out this far?"

Very carefully Rebecca set the skillet on the stove. Unbidden, a face rose in her mind—the face of the son of Bishop Martin, the man at the way station. She turned to study Solali's troubled features. It was some minutes before she could force the words past her stiff lips. When she did, they lacked the humor she tried to put in them. "Solali, are you trying to borrow trouble?"

Solali moistened her lips. "I'm just a'feeling your troubles, wanting to know what you're thinking. Seems, lately, about the time the sun goes down I feel the heaviness starting in you."

Rebecca admitted. "I'm dreading the night. Even on the nights I don't dream, I toss and turn." She brought the pancakes to the table and pushed the sliced tomatoes and honey toward Solali.

"Would it help to ask the Father to take away the dreams?"

When Rebecca could meet Solali's eyes squarely, she said, "Would it? I don't think so."

"Why?" She couldn't answer. There was only Joshua's "Ask!" moving through her being, and she knew he didn't mean to ask for the fear to be gone.

Later as she was finishing the dishes, Solali came in with Joshua's Bible in her hands. "Rebecca, I don't understand these words." She placed the Book in front of Rebecca and touched the verse.

Rebecca read, " 'Whereby are given unto us exceeding great and precious promises: that by these ye might be partakers of the divine nature, having escaped the corruption that is in the world through lust.'" She closed the Book. "Partakers of the divine nature."

"Promises," Solali whispered. "God promising something to us." There was wonder in her voice, for a moment words seemed to fail her, then thoughtfully, "But how can a promise do that?"

Joshua's word was forced out. It was impossible to deny. "Ask."

"It's to be had just for asking? Free?"

"Free." Rebecca's fingers were busy in the pages. She found the place and read it to Solali, but it was really for her own benefit. " 'He that spared not his own Son but delivered him up for us all, how shall he not with him also freely give us all things?' "

"All things."

Could that possibly mean those kinds of things Joshua had been talking about? Like the church bell tolling out, the words rang through her—body, soul, and mind. Like the body, the soul must be free before the mind can be.

There was that blackness inside and Rebecca hugged her arms close, feeling the pull of that one complaining muscle in her shoulder. "It's cold, Solali. I'm going up to bed."

Solali was reading the Bible and there was only the briefest of nods from her.

Once in bed the words returned, *All things, freely, body, soul, mind*. Rebecca tossed restlessly.

And in the morning Solali found her beside the stove, huddled over a cup of tea.

"The dreams?"

She shook her head. Solali poured tea for herself and sat down facing Rebecca. "What is it?"

She felt her grin twist. "I just couldn't sleep."

And after breakfast, Rebecca took a deep breath and knew her resolve was complete. "Solali. I'm going upstairs. Please let me alone. I must settle it—all this—in my mind." Relief blazed through Solali's eyes. Rebecca hesitated. "Do you care? There's washing to be done."

Solali pushed, "No, now go."

Upstairs Rebecca spread the open Bible on the trunk sitting

under the window. She knelt beside it. Through the window she could see the road. A gentle rain had polished the trees and bushes beside it, but in its emptiness, the road looked lonely. It triggered the emotion in her. Far down the way, just tipping the trees, she saw a puff of smoke. That would be the Chambers' home.

She visualized their breakfast table. There would be little Aaron with his tangle of curls dripping porridge down his chin. And Martha. Children. The blackness crept in upon her. Closing her eyes she let it sweep over her. The Bible slipped off the trunk and her weary arms tried to support her head. "Oh, God, why, why?"

The rain ceased and the feeble sunlight touched her. She bent over the Bible and misery kept her thumbing through the pages. Now she remembered the agony of spirit that had sent her into this Book in the beginning. Her wandering fingers found the fifth chapter of Galatians and she read the beginning. " 'Stand fast therefore in the liberty wherewith Christ hath made us free, and be not entangled again with the yoke of bondage.' " Her heart melted as her finger moved down the page and stopped. She read, " 'Ye did run well; who did hinder you that ye should not obey the truth? This persuasion cometh not of him that calleth you.' "

Rebecca's sobs broke into laughter and then ended in tears. "Oh, my kind Lord," she said wiping at the tears. "It's as if You're sitting here beside me, telling me those very words. I'd forgotten how good it is to talk to You, listen to You—these are the very words of God, and I hear You speaking them to me.

"I don't know why I've allowed myself to be led astray, why I've forgotten how good it is to know Your closeness." Abruptly she was silent, and the sure understanding of it all sank in upon her.

The emotions tumbled in. She was caught up in bitterness, loss; she was now twisted beyond reason, captured by rebellion in a dark tunnel of her own making. "It was the moment I blamed You for snatching away my baby. I thought my child was due me. All I did for You, trying to rescue those people. I thought You at least owed me the life of my child."

While she sobbed, prone on the floor with the scrap of rag rug catching her tears, a word moved through her sore mind. "Oh, God, how can I escape?" Escape, a chance to escape. Those were Joshua's words. He had written them in a letter. Then night before last he had given them back to her. The letter? She hadn't re-read the words, the letter had disappeared. Had it been burned? Burn. A firebrand—plucked not from a fire but—the scene filled her mind.

There was that one moment of unbelievable horror before the silence and blackness had claimed her. Plucked.

Rebecca shivered against the rug and feebly tried to force herself up, away from the floor, away from the memory of that scene. "Oh, God, what are You trying to do to me?" *Ask.* With her face buried in the bedquilt, she whispered, "What is it?"

In waiting she felt the quietness creeping into her, stilling her pounding heart, soothing her aching head. She waited; now cradled, upheld, sheltered, and then released.

At that moment she was remembering another scene from the past. It was lighted by a shaft of light pushing through the tent and touching the books on her lap. Outside the willow leaves had fingered the tent like a gentle, inquisitive spirit. A peaceful scene, but there was turmoil inside. Inside the tent, inside Rebecca.

Clearly she recalled the scene, feeling again the struggles of that young woman as she tried to understand the strange forces that were shaking her. "Oh!" Rebecca cried suddenly, seeing that time with brittle, shining clarity. "I was seeking for truth and my lap was full of Mormon books. Why didn't I have the Bible there? That was my moment for finding and there was nothing to be found because, like a horse with blinders on, all the truth was being held away from me while I concentrated on what was in my lap—all those Mormon books.

"For one moment the door was open—that was the moment I questioned." Rebecca whispered. "If I'd said, 'Jesus, show me the way,' I'd probably have run out into the streets of Salt Lake City and straight into the arms of Joshua, 'cause later Ann told me he was there seeking me."

A brand from the burning.

Much later, when the tears had wrung her into limpness and surrender was total, Rebecca was able to speak to her Lord again. "You don't owe me anything. I owe You everything. You are God. You with the nail-pierced hands and the scarred face." She paused and then said slowly and wonderingly, "By Your wounds I am healed. Now my wounds will remind me that You have chosen to rescue me, a brand from the burning. I blamed You for my circumstances. You rescued me."

And then later. "I am healed. I accept You as God, Lord of all of me." She paused. "Now there is my anger." Again she sank beneath the burden. Andrew, Brigham Young. Was it possible to look beyond the hate?

In quietness, she waited. Knowing finally the depths of her hate, seeing the impossibility of escape, knowing her total helplessness, she was wrung into weakness. And then there was hope. She whispered, "Lord Jesus, I need a miracle. That promise. You were delivered up for my death. Now I am dead."

She felt a stirring of life. "You were delivered up for *their* death, too, Andrew's and Brigham Young's, but they don't know it. I know it, I'm *living* in it." Her voice quiet, "I forgive them."

Through her trembling spirit, she stretched out a hand, knowing only total weakness. "The Divine Nature—You. That's the part I need. Fitting me for *life* unto righteousness!"

It was dark when Rebecca walked downstairs. In the kitchen, in the middle of the pool of light from the lamp, Solali sat waiting. Her dark eyes were searching, curious.

Rebecca sat down at the table and spread her hands, palms down. "The blackness is gone. I don't understand how it is possible. It's just simply, totally gone. I'm knowing it is another gift of himself. First He gave me His atonement, now His very life is in me."

Solali whispered, "Is it really possible to live life so close to the Great Spirit that you are held that close, feeling His thoughts, living His love, walking His ways? The Book talks about it here in 1 Corinthians in the second chapter." Now her voice was yearning. "Is it possible this goodness is for anyone who truly searches for it?"

"I think now," Rebecca whispered, "it's all held in that moment when our spirits choose. Do we rebel, or do we live?"

CHAPTER 17

The following day began calmly enough. Rebecca was still moving in the unbelievable circle of serenity. At times she was almost afraid to take too deep a breath, but then there was Solali's wide-eyed joy to remind her of it all. And inside there was that tremulous assurance of yesterday's healing.

The sun shone, the teakettle merrily spouted steam. The fragrance of coffee and toast still clung to the air. Now, with Solali's hands deep in the dishpan and Rebecca wiping the dishes, Solali said, "I've been putting this all together."

She turned to face Rebecca. "Not so much thoughts as feelings. I'm knowing more and more that I'm wanting to go back to my people. There's a big yearning inside of me to help them find this new way of living—not the white man's way but God's way." She stopped and Rebecca knew she was searching out every line of her face, wondering how she was feeling this morning.

"It's still there," she said gently. "And I've never slept so well as I did last night."

"You didn't hear the storm and the wind crashing branches against the house?"

Rebecca shook her head. Turning the plate she was drying, she watched the design of apple blossoms catch the sun. Solali continued, "Our people have need of this message. They must know that the Creator of the heavens and earth loves them. I know their heartache, and it grows worse. I know their loyalties. When they hear about Jesus Christ, and understand, they will be willing to give their hearts to Him.

"Do you understand, Rebecca? When an Indian tears out his heart and offers it up, that's all there is. There's nothing left for him to own. His life is gone and it will all belong to the great God."

Rebecca dropped her towel and turned to Solali. "What a beautiful way to explain it!" With awe in her voice, she repeated. "What beauty! That's what I did. Solali, I tore out my heart and there's nothing left to own. You've understood that all along, and I've just now really grasped it. I—"

There was a shout from the front of the house and the door banged open. Before they could react, Eagle bounded into the kitchen. "Joshua?"

Rebecca was the first to recover. "Why, Eagle! He's gone."

"Gone." With the word, she was seeing that this was no longer the serene face of the Indian she had first met on the mountain. Bewildered, he echoed the word again, "Gone."

Looking at the lines on his face, seeing his agitated pacing of the room, Rebecca knew she must make him understand. "To his pa's place," she touched his arm, "shingles." Understanding swept over his face and now Solali moved. She took her dripping hands out of the dishpan and slowly wiped them on her apron as she spoke softly in the Paiute tongue. Eagle's face cleared. He was nodding and then shaking his head as she reached for the bread. He spun around and headed out the back door.

Solali explained, "He'll take a fresh horse." They were hearing a final shout and the clatter of hooves on the roadway. "I'll go take care of his horse," Solali said.

Rebecca ran to the front door and watched him disappearing down the road. "What's happened? He's terribly upset and he's riding that horse mighty fast." She turned. "Why didn't he eat? It'll take him a good hour to get there, even riding that fast."

"I don't know," Solali said. "He wouldn't tell me, but then I'm feeling he's still angry with me. He said only that he must see Joshua. I'm sure most of his stomping around was just to show me his anger."

"Oh, Solali, I don't believe that."

"But you don't know Eagle. When he left here, I made sure he didn't have a reason to return." She turned and walked back to the kitchen. Rebecca noticed the discouraged droop to her shoulders and didn't know whether to be sad or happy. There were all those things Solali had said just before Eagle came. And now he was gone without even so much as a friendly glance for her.

It was nearly noon when Eagle's horse galloped into the clearing where the neat little cottage stood. The last shingle had been nailed into place. Mr. Smyth had brushed on the last stroke of white paint and Cynthia had polished her windows and settled her kitchen. Joshua was busy loading the shed with a season's supply of firewood.

When he heard the horse, he rested on his axe and waited for the rider to show himself. Now waving his hat he shouted, "Eagle, my friend! We've finished up here and you've arrived just in time for a little celebrating. Ma's frying up a chicken right now." He stopped. Eagle was off the horse now and his face was flinty.

"Josh, we talk." Abruptly he headed for the barn and Joshua followed.

Mr. Smyth was lifting a ladder as they entered and Joshua said, "Pa, you ought not be fooling with heavy things for a while longer. You know I've come just to save you swinging the axe for a few more months. Now, take it easy while you can."

"Why, Eagle," Mr. Smyth's mild voice showed surprise. "I'd thought you'd left us for good." Eagle replied with only a grunt.

Joshua said, "Tell Ma we'll be in later. If the chicken is done, don't wait dinner for us. Eagle has some talkin' to do."

In slow, carefully chosen words Eagle began. "You see fear? Rebecca."

Joshua's head jerked. "She's hurt?"

He shook his head, "No. I see your heart. I know her pain. I know her man, Mormonee." He made a twisting motion with his hands and before Joshua could understand what he meant, he added an eloquent shrug and smote his chest.

"Are you trying to tell me that you know Rebecca's Mormon man and that you don't know what's going on inside of him?" Eagle nodded.

Now he added, "He comes."

Joshua frowned as he studied the Indian's troubled face.

"I'm thinking I don't understand you."

"Here." Eagle's eyes were unwavering.

It was the expression that dropped the fear into Joshua's heart, convincing him of the unthinkable. He rubbed his hands slowly over his face, hoping somehow that his worst nightmare wasn't reality. He paced, then came back to face Eagle. "You're saying that he's coming here. Why?" The dark, inscrutable expression moved across Eagle's face. Joshua was reminded of how little he understood the man. But there was Rebecca, and there were the chiseled features and the cold eyes. There was his obvious fatigue and the winded horse.

"Mormonee come. Bad."

"And I've got to do something about it, but what?" His voice echoed the desperation he was feeling.

Eagle was shaking his head. "Go, take Rebecca."

"Run. You mean he will try to take Rebecca?" Eagle nodded. The lines deepened on his face and slowly he drew his finger across his throat.

"Blood atonement." Horror tightened across Joshua's chest like a paralyzing grip. All of the stories coming out of Utah Territory that he had heard were culminated in Rebecca's terror. He grasped Eagle's shoulders and studied his face. "You're saying this is the man Rebecca lived with. You're saying that he tried to kill her once and that now he comes. Run with Rebecca? Where on God's earth would we run?" He dropped his hands from Eagle's shoulders and paced the barn.

When he stopped before Eagle again, "If he'll follow her clear out here, where would she be safe? We'll spend the rest of our lives running. Do you know what this means? We'll always be knowing that he will yet seek her out and find her."

Again he paced the barn. Disjointed words were tortured out of him. "Eagle, she's nearly out of her mind now. The memories. The nightmares. The hate. I'd hoped she would find the way out. There's this new threat now. He doesn't see—the crazy man doesn't understand that he has no claim on her." Joshua dropped his wildly waving arms and stared at Eagle's impassive face.

"That's it." Joshua stood still. As the realization hit him, he felt calmness sweep over him and he was able to think clearly. "Nowhere in these United States or in these territories is Brigham's doctrine of plural marriage accepted as valid except in the Territory of Utah. In some states the penalty for bigamy is severe. If I could—" He stopped.

The scene of that last night in his own home flashed through his memory. There was Rebecca with the burning, hate-filled eyes, whispering that she would never marry him because of the blackness in her soul. With a groan he turned to pace again. Now his shoulders dropped in defeat.

Eagle's hand fell on Joshua's shoulder. "I kill."

"No." Joshua turned. "Eagle, that's murder and you know it. They'd hunt you down. You'd never escape as long as one man knows what you've done."

"He kill Rebecca." The words were flat. The truth of them was something that Eagle knew as fact. Now Joshua was faced with accepting it.

Joshua walked slowly to the log fence surrounding the manger. He leaned across the logs and scratched the bovine head thrust at him. Through his fear and anger, he felt again the quieting touch. He continued to rub the cow's face and all the impossibilities of the situation began to lose their thrust.

"Seems a body ought to quit trusting his knowledge and let God start directing," he mused. He sucked in his breath and breathed out the prayer. "Father, I believe You're putting this into my mind, and I'm going to have to trust You to work it all out. She's said no pretty strongly. A step at a time. I'll take it and I'll trust You."

He walked back to Eagle. "There's only one way on this earth I can hope to rescue Rebecca from this." Eagle was frowning and Joshua guessed he wasn't understanding all his words. He slowed, speaking carefully. "I'm going to get Rebecca and marry her. He'll have no power on this earth to take her if she's my wife."

"He kill," Eagle warned.

"Will you tell me where he is?"

Eagle nodded and dropped to his knees. With his finger he drew a crude map, showing the trail from Utah. Now lines slashed through the trails, marking the streams and rivers along the route. It was clearly the pattern of rivers and streams cutting out to the Oregon coast. That meant he was in Oregon, working his way up the Applegate trail. Now Eagle touched a spot. "Big settlement."

"City." Joshua said slowly. "Could be Jacksonville, or it could be closer."

"McKenzie."

"He knows the river, the locality," Joshua said slowly. "Have you any idea just where he is now?" Eagle shook his head. "It isn't enough for Rebecca and me to be married right now. She mustn't even be seen by him. For—" He pressed his lips tightly together, thinking now of the effect on her if she were ever to find out that he was in the Territory.

"See," he looked up at Eagle, "we'll have the wedding and everybody around can spread the word that we're married. We'll clear out until he's gone back to Utah."

Eagle frowned. Supposing he didn't understand, Joshua said, "She'll be mine. He'll have no right to her."

Eagle shook his head. "Josh, no understand Mormonee."

Now desperately aware of his need for action, Joshua said, "Eagle, I've got to know just exactly where he is. Will you track him for me?"

He nodded. Bending again to the map, he drew the forks of the McKenzie and the Willamette rivers. Tapping their confluence he said, "Tomorrow, sundown, we meet. I find Mormonee now."

Joshua got to his feet. "Today is Friday. I'll go home and set plans for the wedding. Sunday we'll be married." He turned to Eagle. "Come, eat and rest." Eagle shook his head but Joshua pushed him toward the house.

When Eagle bit into his first piece of chicken, Joshua said, "Ma, Pa, Rebecca and I will be having a wedding this Sunday. Will you drive into town for it?"

Cynthia turned from the stove. "Wedding," she said slowly. "Well, I suppose so. Should give a body a little time to prepare; I don't have a thing to wear."

It was nearly dark when Joshua rode into his own yard. As

he led his mare around the house, he saw Rebecca disappearing into the barn with a milk pail.

The enormity of all that he had planned struck him full force and his heart pounded. "Oh, Lord," he whispered, "You've got to be with me in this. I don't know how I'll handle this. Is it too much to ask that You make her willing?"

Joshua pulled the saddle and bridle from the mare, opened the gate to the corral and slapped her on the rump. He followed Rebecca into the barn.

"Hello, my favorite milkmaid." She straightened and looked over her shoulder. Her face brightened. His heart leaped in response. "If I can talk you into scrambling an egg for me, I'll do the milking. I'm a mite hungry. Only took time for one piece of chicken at noon." She nodded, and he tried to understand the wondering expression in her eyes as she hesitated and then hurried toward the house.

When he entered the kitchen, there were two pairs of eyes to confront. Solali's were nearly as full of questions as Rebecca's. He found himself smoothing his hair self-consciously after he had washed his hands.

When he sat down at the table, Rebecca turned from her task at the stove. "You've caught us short. We didn't expect you home so soon. When there's just the two of us here, we don't do much fussing about what we eat. At least there's a bit of bacon and the bread is fresh."

Solali added, "We're still harvesting tomatoes. This far up the side of the mountain I had been expecting to feel frost long before now. It's still as warm as summer, nearly." She was watching him with that curious expression. Now her question was timid. "Ah—did Eagle see you?"

He nodded. She waited. Rebecca came from the stove, saying, "I've started some dutch cheese. It should be ready to eat by tomorrow." He was still looking at Solali, wondering at her expression. He knew that Eagle's horse had come from here, and now he was guessing that neither Solali nor Rebecca knew his mission. Those were big questions in Solali's eyes, and they were about Eagle.

Solali's eyes met his again and then looked away. "He's fine,"

Joshua muttered, still wondering whether or not he should confide in her. In the end he decided no conversation was better than the evasion that would be necessary if he were to protect Rebecca.

Solali got to her feet. Leaning across the table, she reached for the dishes. "You two go on," she instructed. "I'll be washing up the dishes and then early to bed. I'm—"

"I can't stay," Joshua interrupted hastily. "I'll have a word with Rebecca and then I must be on my way."

"So soon? Where are you going now?" Rebecca asked with a gasp of surprise. Did she seem to be disappointed?

He forced his emotions to quit talking such nonsense. He followed her into the parlor, wondering how she would react when she found out his destination.

He took his time kindling the small fire on the hearth. "I cut a pile of wood for Ma and Pa," he said. "Pa's back still isn't too strong."

Now the fire was crackling and the smoky pine scented the room. He settled back, still reluctant to bring out the words which must be said. He winced thinking of his earlier bravado. Was it totally impossible to think of another way to handle the situation?

Staring into the fire, going over his conversation with Eagle, the memory of the Indian's seething anger touched him. If their exchange of words was limited and unsatisfactory, the man's face, even now, sent fresh new chills through Joshua's heart.

He straightened and turned. Rebecca was sitting on the settle watching him. Framed against the dark wood, her hair gleamed soft and pale. The thought of having her hurt again sent him to her side. "Rebecca." He stopped, surprised by the expression on her face. Her eyes were wide, studying him with an openness and trust he hadn't seen before. Slowly her lips parted and she caught her breath. As if suddenly giving into an earlier resolve, she said, "Joshua—"

"Rebecca," he interrupted roughly. The words must be said and now. The demand must be made before any tenderness would carry him beyond his determination for immediate action. Now. He took a deep breath and met her puzzled expression. "Tomorrow is Saturday. The next day is Sunday—"

"I know." There was that wondering look on her face.

Again he was abrupt, saying, "We're going to be married on Sunday. I've made up my mind and that is how it will be. I love you and you love me. There's no more to be said about the matter. I didn't go all the way to Utah for a sister. I want a wife. Now get that dress out and I'll see you in church on Sunday."

He jumped to his feet and backed toward the door. "I'm sorry. There isn't time to listen to your arguments. Just be there. Ma and Pa are coming down. I'm going now to talk to the parson." His voice was desperate. "Just be there, do you hear?"

"Yes, Joshua."

"What?"

"I said yes, Joshua. I'll be there." He released his breath in an explosion of sound. She frowned and repeated. "Yes. You act like you didn't expect me to say yes."

"I didn't." He stared at her. There was still that open, trusting expression. "You won't change your mind?"

"Do you want me to?"

"No. I just want to be certain that you'll be at the church on Sunday."

"I will."

"Ah, Becky!" He tried to keep the silly grin off his face. She flew to him with her arms open wide. After breathless, silent moments while they clung to each other, Joshua reluctantly released her and started for the door.

"Joshua." Her face was turning upward, now questioning. Her words were whispers. "That letter. Joshua, you said I must ask you what you would do about my wound."

He hesitated, torn, and then there was only that question. Bending over her he cupped her face in his two hands. For a long moment they looked into each other's eyes. In a husky voice, he said, "Becky, my dearest, I will simply kiss the length of that scar, and all the time I'll be thanking the kind Heavenly Father for snatching you and giving you back to me. Always that scar will remind me of how precious your life is to me."

He was nearly to Waltstown before he recovered from his bemused state enough to wonder at the change in Rebecca, and to wonder why he had not thought to ask the reason for it.

Before Joshua had left the parson's home, the town was in an uproar. Best dresses were being hauled to the ironing board. A group of the more accomplished cooks in town were rushed into a hurried conference. Mrs. Norton got out the ham she had been saving for a special occasion.

All heads were bent over the cookbook before Joshua reached the road.

"What's the rush after her puttin' him off all summer?"

"Who said she was?"

"His ma."

"Maybe they caught a young'un a little early."

"Bessie!"

"Well, they have been there alone except for that Indian woman . . ."

"There's no call."

And the next day, just before Joshua reached the fork of the Willamette and the McKenzie, he stopped at the general store. The only new shirt he could find was most certainly a dandy shirt. It was pale blue with tiny dark flowers.

While he eyed it dubiously, the proprietor said, "It's better than a dirty one. Seems to suit you better'n a white one with a collar tighter'n a hangman's noose." He leaned across the counter. "Between you'n me. The missus thinks I can't buy those kind. I'm just guessing I can't sell 'em. But if you really want one, well, Salem's the closest place."

In the end Joshua bought the shirt and let the man talk him into a silk scarf. Then he needed to smell all the soap before he found one that smelled man-like. "Don't want the bees following me," he explained as he paid for the items.

"Only one reason a man would fancy up like that." The proprietor eyed him again. "Too bad I don't have a wedding ring to sell you; bet I could've."

Joshua patted his chest. "I have one of those. About wore it out totin' it around, but it'll do."

When Joshua reached the meeting place, Eagle stepped out

of the bushes. His face was still stern. "Mormonee coming this way. Two days, maybe three. They go slow."

"Another day or so and people will know who he's a'looking for," Joshua said, adding bitterly, "And they'll be giving out information, thinkin' he's a long-lost buddy."

Eagle led him through the bushes, away from the pounding water. There he had built a fire. A salmon was impaled on sticks and cooking slowly. He pointed to the bed of skins. "Rest. You go in the morning and I go back to trail."

Joshua nodded. "I've pretty well covered this section. Gentle-like, I've let it be known I'd be obliged if folks were a little tight-lipped about me." With a weary sigh he dropped to the skins. "If I'm out of here by dawn, I'll be to the church in plenty of time."

Eagle's eyes were full of curiosity, and Joshua guessed that his grin was telling him more than the words. "She's going to marry me. Tomorrow morning at the church. The whole town will be there."

Early the next morning, Eagle stood on the bank of the McKenzie. For once his face was lighted with a grin of pure delight as he watched Joshua.

"Aw!" Joshua split the water howling in misery. " 'Tis mighty cold."

Eagle had the fire going, but he was still shaking his head. "Wedding," he grunted. He studied the shirt before he handed it to Joshua.

"I'll buy you one like it if you'll get married." Joshua was surprised to see the fleeting shadow cross Eagle's face. He turned away as he combed his pale hair, saying casually, "Did you know she sent Matthew a'packin'? I think you've read her wrong." Joshua wasn't certain Eagle understood, but he did see the expression on the man's face soften.

Before Joshua reached the outskirts of Waltstown, he heard the church bell. This was no terse reminder of Sabbath worship. The bell rang loud and long, with a touch of excitement that reached Joshua. He reined his horse on the last rise and watched the wagons moving briskly down the road.

CHAPTER 18

Solali reported, "Mr. Chambers says he'll be along to take you into town to the church. The parson told him to come." She followed Rebecca around the house as Rebecca's restless feet carried her from parlor to kitchen. "You've scarce eaten a bite of breakfast; that's no way to begin your wedding day."

"Did you check again to see if we got all the wrinkles out of the wedding dress?"

" 'Tis fine." Solali added wistfully, "A beautiful dress it is. Silk and all, with the beautiful pink flowers on it—it'll be the finest dress seen in this town."

Rebecca turned abruptly and clasped Solali's hands. She was blinking away the tears. "Oh, Solali. I've been so caught up with thinking about Joshua, and being in such a rush to be ready for today, that I've scarce given the dress a thought. Do you know this is the fulfillment of a dream I've had since I was a wee girl? I still remember my mother talking about her wedding. Those memories draw such a beautiful picture. I'm believing that now there'll be an even stronger link between us when I can stand before that parson and marry Joshua wearing her dress. How I thank God now that He didn't let me have the wedding dress before—"

She was silent while the dark thoughts threatened her; then she lifted her head. " 'Tis the love of Jesus wrapping it all, and that's all I'll concentrate on. The love of Jesus making right out of it all."

She moved restlessly. "Do you think I should start dressing now?"

"It's not much past sunup."

"I wonder where Joshua had to go?" Solali could only shake her head. "You're worrying about Eagle, aren't you?"

Solali sighed. " 'Tis strange. Did you notice that it was his horse Joshua was riding when he left? And Joshua was a mite agitated, not like a man just going a'visiting. I'm feeling Eagle's up to something."

"In trouble or hurt, that's what you're thinking?" Rebecca looked questioningly at Solali, but she turned away with a shrug.

Solali paced to the parlor windows and back. "Seems we best get you into that dress. Those buttons will take all day. I've never seen that many buttons to hold together any kind of dress, not to mention a wedding dress. I 'spect it was a miracle your folks ever managed to have you."

"Oh, Solali!" Rebecca, embarrassed, smiled and shook her head in mock horror. "But you are right, there's lots. I've a buttonhook somewhere; that'll help."

When Solali finished the last button, she turned Rebecca. "Ah, there, you look like an angel. The little pink posies on the bodice are all the flowers you need." She touched the deep lace ruffles at the sleeves and the ones cascading down from the shoulders into a deep V at the waistline.

"Are there spots where I cried all over it?" Rebecca asked anxiously, peering over her shoulder.

"No. But that wad of hair is all wrong. Come, let me brush the curls loose." Lifting Rebecca's hair high, Solali brushed the softly curling locks around her finger and pinned the cascade of curls high off her neck.

There was a shout from the front of the house and Solali dropped the brush. "Oh, it's the Chambers; it's time to leave."

Rebecca stood motionless and Solali reached for her hand. "No, don't even stop to think."

"The Bible. I must have my Bible." She whirled around and picked it up as Solali gathered up their shawls. Together they hurried down the stairs.

When they reached the edge of town, Rebecca's trembling hand touched Mr. Chambers' sleeve. "Please," she pleaded, "Don't go so fast. I—"

"You have cold feet like all the rest. Never you mind, just don't think now." Mrs. Chambers turned to smile at her over the baby's head. "Besides, we're nearly late. Do you want Joshua to think you've changed your mind? He might just choose a lass out of the congregation. When a man makes up his mind to wed, don't you be slowin' him down."

"Whoa." Mr. Chambers was halting the team in front of the little white church. Aaron jumped out and called, "Come on, everybody, let's go to the wedding!"

Slowly Rebecca climbed out of the wagon and followed Solali into the church. Suddenly shy, she clutched the Bible against her. Head down, she walked with reluctant little steps.

The buzz of conversation ceased as she reached the door, but until she reached the first line of pews, she dared not lift her head.

They were all standing and all eyes were studying her. In front of the altar, with the sunshine streaming across his shoulders, Joshua waited. When she met his gaze, he sighed with relief and a grin spread across his face.

Beside Joshua, the song leader, wearing his cutaways, stood on tiptoe and lifted his arm. "Let's sing." The organist crashed down on the chords, and as Rebecca walked toward Joshua the congregation sang, "Praise God, from whom all blessings flow . . ."

Parson Williams stepped forward as the skirts rustled into place in the pews. "Dearly beloved, we are gathered here in the sight of God and man—" Joshua gripped her hand and the words faded as she looked up at him. Now his hand tightened and she heard Parson Williams saying, "I charge you, if either of you know any reason why this marriage should not be solemnized, then confess it now. In the sight of God, you must be lawfully joined together."

And through the silence, he spoke again. "Joshua, will you take this woman to be your wife?"

Rebecca caught her breath as he turned to face her. His voice was deep and clear, "I do. I take you, Rebecca Ann Wolstone, to be my wife."

With a gentle smile, she said, "And I take you, Joshua Smyth.

I promise to love, to honor, and obey—"

Now in the final moment, Joshua struggled with the scarf about his neck and the ring on its rawhide thong was awkwardly pulled out. Carefully he got his pocket knife and cut the leather. In a voice raised nearly to a shout of triumph, Joshua said, "Rebecca, with this ring I wed you. For as long as we both shall live, I pledge my love and loyalty to you."

"Joshua," came the chant from the congregation. "You're married; you can kiss the bride."

And in the din, Rebecca turned to the parson. "Please—" she opened her mother's Bible and grasped Joshua's shirtsleeve— "please, we must write our names here. See the place?" Then she shook back the lace ruffles as Parson Williams brought the pen and bottle of ink. There was her shaky signature and Joshua's firm hand signing beside her.

The church bell began pealing out the news. From hand to hand and kiss to kiss, Rebecca and Joshua were moved toward the door. "The wedding cake. Cut the cake," someone called.

"Now, you just wait," came the answer; "there's chicken and ham first. 'Sides, it isn't your weddin'."

The noonday sun made Rebecca blink. She wiggled her shoulders under its warmth. "Oh, what a beautiful, blessed day for a wedding!"

Down the steps, propelled by the force of the crowd, they moved toward the trees and the picnic tables. Joshua's hand firmly clasped her elbow. "Let's get out of here. Let's leave. With all that food they'll never miss us."

"Joshua, we'll hurt their feelings. Let them have their fun." She tried to understand his frown, but they had reached the table and plates were thrust at them.

And the cake. As she moved around it she noticed Joshua's dogged expression, his hurried glance. Amusement curved her lips into a smile. He was expecting tricks. She captured his hand and guided it with the knife through the cake.

"Get him good, smear that icing!"

She was still smiling at Joshua when she became aware of the growing silence. With a tiny fragment of sticky cake still in her hand, she turned, gasped.

Joshua was pushing her aside, moving in front of her. Her faltering hand flattened the cake against the table and she leaned heavily against Solali. In a distant dream she heard Joshua's demanding, "What brings you here?"

"I've come to claim my wife."

The gasp was collective, the murmur of horror grew as the crowd stepped back. Now there was only Andrew Jacobson facing Joshua Smyth. Even in the pain, Rebecca was aware of the slash of blackness. From frown, to hair, to coat; his darkness was aligned against the brightness of Joshua.

Andrew moved first. His casual glance took in the food, the cake, and then sought the authoritative figure. "Parson," his voice was mocking, "am I seeing a wedding party in progress?" He turned slowly to meet the eyes of those men and women staring at him. "This ought not to be," he said gently but totally in command. Andrew Jacobson, leader of men, was in top form.

He turned to Rebecca. "Rebecca, my dear, surely you remember our wedding. Not as grand as this—but it came first."

Joshua moved, saying impatiently, "Jacobson, you have no legal claim on Rebecca Wolstone. Now, just this day, in the sight of God and man, we were united as husband and wife."

Andrew faced the crowd. Where Joshua's voice was taut with strain, his was soft, even and low. "Now you good people honor God's commandments, don't you?" He glanced up at the steeple on the church, paused and said, "Don't you believe the Constitution of the United States of America guarantees a man the right to practice his religion in freedom, without the government interfering?"

The nods were collective. The eyes still curious, they were fastened on Andrew Jacobson, not Rebecca and Joshua.

"Freedom of religion is one thing, but—"

Jacobson's voice cut through Joshua's. Turning to Rebecca he said kindly. "You can't deny, can you, that a marriage took place and that a divorce never did?" Pressing her trembling hands against her temples, she shook her head. "And how long did you live with me as my wife?" She moistened her lips. Now an edge of impatience in his voice, he demanded, "Speak up."

"Three years," she whispered.

"And did I ever give you grounds to leave that marriage?" She opened her mouth and he snapped, "Within the confines of our religion?"

"Jacobson!" Joshua cried, "you are twisting it—the whole picture! What about last year—what about—"

"You're accusing—" His voice ripped through Joshua's. His face was icy cold as his glance shifted between Rebecca and Joshua. "What about it? Remember, these are accusations. You had better be prepared to provide evidence. If you intend to deliver accusations which will blacken my name, my reputation, you'd better be ready to substantiate them."

Without a pause he wheeled to face the crowd, his coat parting to reveal the gun strapped to his waist. He raised his hand, the crowd hushed and attentive before him. "Whom will you believe, a wronged husband or a conniving debaucher of innocent women—a perverter of marriage and religion? My good people, in the name of all that's holy, whom will you believe?"

Parson Williams' face was ashy. He stepped forward. "Sir, in all good faith I performed this ceremony. That it was conducted in a hasty manner, I can't deny. Joshua assured me that it—it was all on the up and up." He cleared his throat nervously under the righteous gaze bent upon him. "Under the circumstances—" he said weakly.

"Wait!" Joshua cried, taking a hasty step toward the parson. There was a restraining hand on his sleeve and he shook it off. "Will you not hear me out?" he pleaded. "Rebecca was tricked." There was a collective murmur from the people and Joshua's words were lost in the growing uproar as he said, "It was a marriage that wasn't a true marriage."

Jacobson's voice rose above the clamor. "She lived with me, knowing the teachings of our religion and the commands divinely given. She knew that we were obligated to honor our god through this marriage."

"But she left that religion." Joshua's statement was heard as the crowd again quieted.

"She has obtained no divorce."

"There can be no divorce when there has been no marriage."

"Are you besmirching the name of this woman? Are you calling her a prostitute?"

The crowd roared and Joshua shouted, "Defend your claims in court! I say you are wrong. Come back tomorrow and we'll find a lawyer together."

"And leave my wife in your hands?" The heads were shifting from one man to the other. Beside Rebecca, Solali gasped. Rebecca raised her face. The expressions turned toward her were hostile. An angry hiss rose.

"No!" Joshua shouted. "I will not allow you to leave here with Rebecca."

"My good man," the parson spoke slowly. "It seems to me that this gentleman has a prior claim. I suggest you not fight his rights. In the name of good religion, and all that's holy, if you must have her, be just and fair. Let him have his day in court."

Joshua moved quickly, but more quickly came the words, "Grab him!" Horror filled Rebecca as she watched Joshua slump under the blow. Now Andrew's hand was reaching toward her.

He passed his gentle smile around the circle and then addressed her. "Come, my dear. All's forgiven. We'll see these good people later."

"I'll not go with you." She raised her chin and stepped backward. Glancing quickly around, she begged, "Please help me." Solali tried to hold her but strong arms were hindering her. Rebecca saw the mood of the crowd and crumpled. "There's no one who will believe?"

She looked from face to face and saw the bewilderment, the pursed lips, the veiled glances. She met Cynthia's eyes and watched her turn away. "My poor son!" she cried, hiding her face against her trembling husband as he bent over Joshua.

"Ma'am," Parson Williams spoke slowly to Rebecca. "You have admitted he is your husband. There is not one thing we legally can do to stop him."

Numbness pricked at Rebecca's face and body. She was barely conscious of Andrew's grasp as he lifted her onto his horse. Parson Williams' words continued to press upon her. They were the only link with consciousness. "Nothing we can do. Sorry."

Andrew's horse was galloping away from the quiet group clustered in the churchyard. Desperately Rebecca clung to the saddle horn in front of her and forced her body away from Jacobson's. His arms tightened about her while the loathing shivered through her.

Chuckling, he said, "Now stop, little one, stop acting like that. You didn't think I would give up once I discovered you were still alive?"

"Steven Martin?" she forced through stiff lips.

"Yes, our dear faithful friend, Steven."

Helpless anger began to well up inside and Rebecca spoke through clenched teeth. "It cannot be love that brings you to Oregon after me. Isn't it more truthful to say you are fearful of what I might reveal, and that your intentions haven't changed in the past year?"

"What is it you're saying?" His voice was mocking. "Why, Rebecca, my darling wife, you don't think I'd allow a rift in my celestial kingdom, do you?"

"Do you really believe that, or is it all just a pretense to which you cling?"

"Hush now. Tell me where you live. We need to get your clothes and a horse for you. Where will we find the baby?"

The strange, twisted scene suddenly became real. The baby was the link. All those hard facts about the baby lay like stones upon her heart. Her silence made him impatient. He hostled her arm. "Speak up. You'll not even consider leaving him behind. After all, he's my son." The gun was pressing against her back, but it was his hand now grasping her arm and painfully forcing it up behind her, twisting her in the saddle until he could meet her eyes, that made her cry out. Through the pain his expression burned life back into her.

"I'll not tell you anything. Let's just see how long this mare will last with the two of us on her."

"We aren't going anywhere until we get my son." The words rebounded in Rebecca's mind. Her thoughts were full of the picture of Joshua in pursuit and she knew she must stall. She pressed her lips together. He twisted her arm further. "My son."

Now with tears streaming down her face, tears of pain and

anger, she cried, "There is no son! Andrew, you killed your child last year. I wish to God that I'd had the wits to say it all to those people. I still can't believe they were so twisted by your half-truths." He jerked her arm and the thrust of pain forced her into silence.

She knew the horse had slowed, but her tortured mind couldn't supply a reason. "My son," again he repeated, this time with a hint of uncertainty. The gun was now pressed against her face.

Terror filled her completely. But with a broken sob, she managed to say, "You'll never believe me, and there's not one thing you can do to prove me wrong or right. You might go back and ask those people. They know there is no child. I challenge you to return. By now they may have their heads." Now with mockery in her voice she cried, "Ah, Andrew, don't I hear their horses?"

For a moment there was uneasiness in his eyes and he released her arm and jerked the horse's reins. " 'Tis a shame, but your precious wedding dress will be a rag before we reach Utah." He cracked his reins across the horse. "Very well, my dear, then you'll have to make the best of the matter." His voice was again smooth and assured.

His arm tightened, cruelly biting into the scar tissue down her side. With the strange detachment shock brings, Rebecca thought of last September and reminded herself it could happen again. Clenching her fist against her throat, she felt the smoothness of the wedding ring and glanced down.

How brightly it gleamed in the sunshine. Did she dare read symbols in that bright circle of light? Was hope possible? She knew with the springing assurance that as certainly as Joshua had sought her and given her the ring, he would not rest until he found her again. Would he find her in time? She shivered and tried to pray.

They had been riding for an hour when Rebecca began to recognize her surroundings. Did he know where he was going? The narrow trail he had been following twisted behind Walts-town up the mountains. They were now directly east of Joshua's section. She knew the area was uncharted and unmarked except for these trails used by the woodcutters. Only crude shelters and high mountains lay before them.

For a moment she toyed with the thought of escape, but how easy it would be to become lost in the dense forest. How treacherous the rocky slopes were with their hidden ravines. How frightening the night and lurking creatures of the dark. She felt that arm fastened around her and was reduced to trembling panic.

But then she took a deep breath and tried to forget the trembling. There was an equal danger. She said, "No man in his right mind would try to cut through this country." Slowly she said, "I've been hearing tales of the cutting of Barlow Pass. That's just north of here; cuts through the Cascades just south of The Dalles. When those folks first crossed the mountains, their very lives depended on slashing their way through. They nearly didn't make it. Half dead when they reached the valley."

He didn't comment. She took his silence as indecision, and hope came newborn. Rebecca found she could pray. She whispered, "Father, O Father, please let Joshua find the way."

When he slowed the horse at the first tangle of bush, she cried, "You realize, don't you, once you get over these mountains you must cross eastern Oregon Territory? The Meekers' train nearly perished, and they had some idea of where they were going."

"And you think I don't?" She was hoping that was uncertainty she was hearing in his voice. They reached another trail and when he turned on it, he spurred the horse confidently.

They were climbing, first east and then north. Now the sun was slanting across the top of the coastal range and Rebecca guessed the afternoon was far spent. Desperate now, she looked around, trying to recall all that she had been told about the area.

That it was densely wooded, she need not be told. They had climbed high above the valley. She did remember that the men felled timber here and snaked it back down to the valley behind their teams. Had Matthew and Joshua come this far to cut wood?

She felt hope die when she reminded herself of the obvious.

How would Joshua guess where to look? For that matter, what chance had he of recovering from that blow on the head in time to look before every trace of their passing was covered?

Thinking back to that scene at the church, she remembered the expression on Cynthia's face and, momentarily, bitterness threatened to sweep over her. The stigma was a taint which would follow her the rest of her life.

Now, like an audible command, the words filled her mind: " 'Stand fast in the liberty . . .' " And while bitterness and futility fought for control, there was that command filling her with direction and peace.

She realized Andrew was guiding the horse off the path. He said, "We're nearly there." Through the trees she saw a tiny log cabin.

As they approached she realized it was very old. When he stopped the horse and slid off, she sat studying it. Its one window was broken and the roof sagged. A twig and mud chimney poked broken remains through the roof.

"Why have you forced me to come with you?" she asked, making herself look at him.

"Because you are mine, part of my kingdom. And also, my dear, you must learn discipline and self-control. You must now earn your right to be part of my household—my eternal household. You will do so by serving the other wives."

She stared at him, studying the familiar face, remembering the hate which had warped her for so long. She rubbed her hands wearily across her face as the disappointment and grief welled up within. How could she possibly endure? Wasn't that hate threatening again? What happened to that sweet peace, the freedom?

"Dear God," she was murmuring in fearful desperation now as she watched him move around the building, examining the ground and checking the sagging fence at the rear of the house. "Please, Father," she pleaded, "I thought I was free of it all— the black things. Now they're coming back more ugly than ever." She thought of a break for freedom on the horse, but remembered the gun in time.

In the quiet moment, while his footsteps receded and the

sun-warmed pine scented the air around her, she became conscious of the fearful anxiety loosening its grip. Now set apart, released, she had one glad moment to realize she was fearing not Andrew but the blackness which had previously filled her soul for so long. Now she knew the blackness wasn't inside any more, only outside. And she would not let it in.

In wonder, she sat experiencing the truth while she measured the value of it. She was healed. She was free from the awful, consuming hate. That experience was real, more real than the horror of this present time. The wonder was back in her life as she whispered, "He answered my prayer."

She fell to musing about it. Through surrender to the Spirit, and by asking and accepting, the miracle had happened.

Andrew came around the house and opened the door. Slowly she slid off the horse and followed him into the house. She saw the bundle dangling from the rafters and watched him untie the rope and pull it free. "I see the 'coons and rats couldn't reach my larder. We'll have dinner as soon as you can get it ready." He went to spread the blankets across the shelf bed built into the wall of the cabin.

Turning away from the dismal, dirty room, she went to lean against the doorjamb. Far to the west the sun sparkled on a thread of the McKenzie. "We must be on the top of the mountain," she murmured. The haze of woodsmoke was in the air. It was someone's supper fire far below. Just possibly it could be the Chambers or the Bakers. They would be busy preparing their evening meal, already forgetting the events of the day. Where would Joshua be? And his ma and pa. Her aloneness bit into her, and she squeezed her arms tight against her body, refusing the weakness that demanded tears. Concentrating on taking deep, slow breaths, she pushed the pictures out of her mind and accepted the stretch of the unknown lying just ahead.

A sentence from far out of the past moved into her thoughts. It had been one of those long-ago verses which had carried no meaning until just last night when she had found and read the words.

Aloud now, spurred by the memory-picture Andrew painted when he said "serve the wives," she whispered, " 'Know ye not, that to whom ye yield yourselves servants to obey, his servants ye are? . . .' " Last night she had read those words and rejoiced in her freedom. Tonight—she winced but plunged bravely on with the thought—she *was free.* Jesus Christ had won her freedom.

She lifted her face against the musty, decaying wood and whispered, "I promised to obey you, Lord. Please help me keep that promise." With her eyes still closed she rested and her breathing grew calm and even.

Clearly now, from deep inside, she was thinking and moving deliberately. Surrender to her Lord? Of course. Conscious acceptance that He was here and at work in her, more powerful than herself, than Andrew. Slowly she opened her eyes, saw the moldy wood and heard the crackle of fire behind her.

She turned. On his knees before the pack, having at least momentarily given up on her cooperation, Andrew pulled out the food and dishes and began arranging them on the wooden bench. Now she was seeing his proud figure and arrogant face in a new light. At one time she had thought it impossible to rise above the hate and fear this man inspired; now she was knowing a new fact: She no longer trembled in his presence; he was just a man.

Jesus Christ died for this man, just as surely as He had died for her. Did Andrew know that?

He beckoned. There was a meal to be reckoned with. He fed the fire while she mixed the pancakes and divided the jerky. Strange rite. The old familiar patterns but now changed. It was as if she stood apart, no longer caught in the turmoil of that woman who had been his wife. She held up the apples. "Oregon apples? They're nicer than Utah's."

CHAPTER 19

Joshua moved and groaned. A cool cloth pressed against his face. Nat Chambers was on his knees beside him. "Sorry, my friend," he was shaking his head regretfully. "How a man can get himself into so much trouble is beyond me! Sometimes a fella needs to be protected from himself."

Joshua's mother pressed the cloth against the lump, her lips pursed into a thin line. "I had a bad feeling about it all along. 'Twer mostly because you were so secret-like."

Solali dropped to her knees beside the two of them and touched Mrs. Smyth's arm. "Please, you're not—"

Mrs. Smyth interrupted her, "Now you just keep quiet. 'Tis easy to see you was stickin' up for her all along. Bet you been pushin' this affair from the beginning."

"Joshua," Solali wailed, "make them understand."

He groaned. "I've tried." He touched his jaw and the lump on the back of his head, struggling to sit up.

Nat said aplogetically, "I think you hit your head on the edge of the table. I aimed only to get your mind off going after that dude. He was wearin' a gun!"

Solali turned to the rim of faces. "Doesn't that tell you something? Don't you see? It's bad, not good. These kinds of marriages. Even the government says so."

"Ya mean the kind Rebecca had with him?" Baker asked slowly, jerking his head toward the empty road.

Joshua pushed himself to a sitting position, cradling his head. "It's illegal. If the same thing happened anywhere else

175

in the country, they'd a' run them outta town."

"That's just what was happening back east. Illinois and New York." Chris Evans was speaking from the back of the crowd. "Back there they was keepin' those activities mighty secret for fear of the government. But news leaks and that's one of the reasons things were so hot for them."

"No place," Solali added, "recognizes these marriages except Utah Territory."

"I'm not understandin' what you're saying." Mrs. Chambers pushed her way through the group. "What's illegal? What's goin' on?"

Joshua raised his head. "Rebecca married Andrew Jacobson, thinking he was a single man. It turned out that he was already married and had a family. In any place but Utah that's called a bigamous marriage and it's not only illegal but it can cause a heap of trouble for the guy caught in it. The second marriage just plain doesn't exist in the eyes of the law. In Utah these kinds of marriages are not only tolerated, they're encouraged. It's the teachings of the church."

"And just what does all this make Rebecca?" Mrs. Norton's voice was belligerent. "We've no call to be sucked into accepting a bad woman in the town. This is an honest, law-abiding place. We don't want no bad women."

Solali dropped her head. "You don't understand. Rebecca *didn't know* he was already married! And after she found out— well, I—Rebecca and I were both members of the church. When Brigham Young tells you to do something, you aren't allowed to think for yourself; you just do it."

"You're saying you were one, too?" Lettie Depoe whispered. "I'd never have guessed. You seemed to be so nice."

Joshua raised his head. "Mrs. Depoe, if your husband came home and said that Parson here told him that he had to take another wife in order for you all to have a position in the here-after, would you fight it?"

"I'll say I would!" she said indignantly; then she cocked her head, slowly saying, "You mean that's the way it goes? . . . Maybe I wouldn't , especially if I could see others doing it. You say they believe *God's* putting it up to them?" She settled back on her chair and said, "My, how could that man lead them astray? Why, there's nothing in the good Book to let you think—"

"Might be easy to swallow, if'n you let someone else do the thinking for you." Little Mrs. Crocket was speaking. "I've heard all kinds of tales. Seems a body could get sucked in deeper and deeper. Where do you call an end to taking what they say as gospel?"

Mrs. Hanson spoke up, " 'Tis a danger. Always. A person needs to know just what the good Book says, and then keep on stuffing the words inside him so's he'll never get confused or led astray when someone comes along with a fancy teaching.

Now Clarence Norton demanded, "Yes, but where do we call an end to all this? What does it make this little girl, Rebecca? Did I hear you say that a divorce isn't possible?"

"There's been no legal marriage," Joshua repeated simply. "He was already married to another woman. In the eyes of his church he did no wrong. The church will recognize as many marriages as he wants to make. But let one of these women step outside the Territory, and you know just how society sees her."

"And you knew all this and still wanted to marry her?"

"Where's *your* religion, Norton?" Hollis Evans demanded. "Didn't you hear the Parson's sermon last week? He said we're not to judge. He said we're to forgive and live in love. If that's what Joshua has done, that's what we're to do."

Joshua tried to get to his feet and Cynthia held him down. "Wait a minute, son. If I hear you right, your intentions are to bring a tattered lily into my home, soiled."

"It isn't your home, Ma, it's mine," he said simply without rancor. While they stared at each other, the conversation continued around them.

"What about the story in the New Testament about the woman taken in adultery and Jesus sayin' that the guy without sin could cast the first stone? What of it?"

"Well, I really like Rebecca. Sweet little thing like that! She's had a hard life of it. I'm for sayin' I'd like her to be part of this community and I'd be proud to call her my friend." Mrs. Baker pushed her hair out of her eyes and juggled her toddler.

Joshua got to his feet and stood swaying.

"Where are you going?" Abe demanded.

"I'm going to find my wife. And I'm lookin' until I do, even if I have to track that guy clear to Utah."

"Hey, she really *is* Joshua's wife, isn't she, Parson?"

Cynthia stood beside Joshua. With arms akimbo she said, "Whose idea was it, all this keeping quiet about her past?"

"It doesn't matter now," he said flatly. "But I guessed that this is just what was bound to happen. I knew you all would be judgin' her and pointin' your fingers if you knew. I was hoping the facts would never come out. I hoped that she could recover from the pain of her past and that then we could be married. Now there's this. God only knows the fear and anguish she's feelin' right now." His eyes met Solali's and he read the answering horror in her eyes.

"Then you pushed having the wedding today for a reason," Parson Williams leveled a stern look at Joshua. "I'm guessing you got wind that he was coming." He paced an anxious step back and forth in front of Joshua. "Young man, if you'd told me the whole story, I'd have sent the man packing and you'd have your wife."

As Joshua reached his hand toward the man, the sound of hooves beating on the hard-packed road broke the silence that now held the group. "It's someone coming fast." They surged to the road.

The man was off the horse and racing through the cloud of dust. "Eagle!" Joshua and Solali gasped together.

Joshua could see Eagle's face was lined with fatigue and the panting, snorting animal he rode told more of the story. Now he saw the face Eagle lifted to Joshua was filled with sorrow and his puzzled eyes were searching Joshua's. "Moved last night." He hesitated. There was still that questioning expression as he glanced around at the silent crowd of people. Seeing the ruins of the dinner and the cake with its one missing piece, he turned quickly and his anxious hand grasped Joshua. "She not go—willing?"

"What do you know?" Joshua stepped closer.

"I saw—" he motioned toward the road and then pointed to the mountains—"I follow and—almost I stop them." Now he shrugged.

"Do you know where they are now?" Joshua was speaking intently, slowly, hoping the man was understanding every word. "Can you lead us to them?" Eagle was nodding and Joshua spun around. "Ma, Pa, Solali, I'm going after her."

"Not alone. You stand no chance alone." It was the parson speaking, but Norton and Baker chimed in and other voices were added to the protest.

"We're all going. That's the least—"

"A fresh horse for Eagle!" Joshua was yelling as he ran for his horse. Quickly saddles were thrown on and cinches jerked impatiently. Already Eagle was plunging ahead of the others. "Up the mountain?" Joshua questioned, "Eagle, are you sure?"

There was only that brief nod and the men spurred their horses after him.

Over an hour had passed before Eagle reined in and lifted his hand. "This far I follow."

"There's not much of a trail up this way," Chambers said slowly. "We're pretty close to the road and we've all cut up this trail just ahead when we've gone to cut wood. Seems off to the north there's a tumble-down cabin. Somewhere just beyond that the trail ends. If they try to cut through to the crest, they'll have a hard time of it. It'll be a fight every inch of the way. One thing, if he's really come this way, there's no hope of their keepin' ahead of us. There's no way he can cut through the bush that fast; the stuff's thicker'n a hedge."

"Likewise," Norton was speaking now, "we'll be bogged down and lose time a'fightin' our way over and all for nothin' if'n he's *not* come this way."

"Aw," Evans added, "why'd a man come this way in the first place?"

"He'd be taking that trail because he didn't know better or else 'cause he's afraid of being chased."

Parson Williams spoke up, "Afraid? That doesn't sound like an honest man." Joshua jerked his reins impatiently, not knowing whether to be glad because the man was seeing light, or angry because he still questioned.

Eagle was off again with Norton riding beside him. The sun was slipping behind the coastal range and the sky flared yellow. "Not much of daylight left." Thane Hanson spoke behind Joshua. The horses slowed to a walk as they fought their way through the tangle of maple vine and huckleberry bushes. Rhododendron and scrub fir bound them like grasping arms. "Seems we ought to stop and make some plans," he continued. "These trails are bad after dark. 'Tis easy even for a good horse to go over the side, bein' he can't see through the bushes either."

"There's time for talk when we know where they are." Joshua's voice was rough. With the press of nighttime, Rebecca's terror-stricken face filled his thoughts.

From the shadows ahead came the night owl's call. "Hold it," Joshua snapped, "that's Eagle. Wait up."

He circled his mount and the men closed in. Now Eagle was in their midst. "Cabin. I smell smoke. Hobble horses, we walk."

"When we get close we'll have to fan out," Joshua muttered. "If we're right about him runnin', we'll never catch him otherwise. Watch your feet; he'll have a sharp ear cocked."

They moved out silently, carefully. When the straight, sharp shadow of the cabin roof was their horizon, they stopped. Norton moved close to Joshua.

"What if he's holdin' a gun on her?"

Joshua turned his face toward the man. Through clenched teeth he muttered, "This is my game now and there'll be no need of words with him." Joshua felt Eagle's hand on his arm and was silent.

"We move around cabin," Eagle whispered; "we wait."

CHAPTER 20

Rebecca paced the tiny cabin; back and forth she went across the broken boards and stretches of packed earth floor. The chill of the mountain air moved in the broken window. But with a curt shake of her head, she rejected the blanket Andrew held toward her.

"That's a right pretty dress," he drawled. "Too bad you didn't see fit to wear it to the ball. Remember the ball?" At her silence he continued, "You'd have been the belle of that ball because of the dress. Even Brigham's wives couldn't have outdone you. Imported lace, huh?" She still didn't answer but turned to pace again. "Might as well sit down; it could be a long, cold night."

"Just what are your plans?"

"East. Just move east even if it's only a mile a day. When we hit the cutoff we'll be safe."

"What do you mean, safe?"

"Well, I'm expecting your fella will be coming out with a gang."

She turned to look at him and caught the brooding expression in his eyes. "You don't really want me, do you?" she whispered. There was no answer and she continued, "Why don't you just let me go? The child would have been the only possible reason for you to come after me and now—" She couldn't go on for a moment and then she whispered, "If you ever did love me, why not allow me to have my happiness now?" He didn't answer and she continued to pace.

When he finally spoke his voice was heavy. "Rebecca, you've

wearied me in the past with your rebellion. When will you settle yourself to accept things as they are?" She stared at him, realizing the futility of any thought or reasoning outside of that which he chose to believe.

The fire was burning low and the nighttime chill was creeping into the cabin. Andrew got off the bench and lifted a log toward the fire. "It's a wonder you don't burn the place down," she said. "There's chinking constantly falling into the fire. But then go ahead. About the time the roof catches fire, those down in town will begin to wonder who's up here."

Andrew stopped and looked at her for a moment. A worried frown creased his forehead as he said, "Could be. Might be a good idea to check out that chinking before I shove more wood on."

He dropped to his knees and leaned across the dying fire to peer up the chimney. The gun holster tipped and her attention was caught. Without thought or design, two quick steps put her behind him. Again he leaned and she bent over him. A gentle shove with her left hand and her right hand had the gun.

"What in the name—" Soft ash flew, but he recovered his balance and got to his feet.

Back across the room, Rebecca watched him. Her breath was coming in quick hard gasps, but the gun she held was steady and it pointed at the white spot of his shirt. Even in the dimness of the room, she could see the color leave his face. He started to take a step and then hesitated.

"That *is* a good idea, Andrew," she said. Her voice was very soft, but she knew he heard. "Now, put your hands out so's I don't get nervous."

He tried to laugh but it was strained. "Rebecca, my dear, that gun is loaded, you best—"

"I'd already figured it was loaded, and you would have used it, wouldn't you? I know you would. There's last year to remember." Now she was silent, watching him, seeing the real fear in his eyes. Suddenly there was the sickening terror of last year moving through her. The cries of the children, wide-eyed and clinging, pressing about her. Could she be hearing again the women with ashen faces as their sounds of agony split through the night air? The gun trembled in her hands and she looked down at it, now fully aware of what she had done. She was holding Andrew's gun and if she pulled the trigger, she would kill him.

"Rebecca." His voice was still taut with strain. "Please put that gun down and let's talk."

"Andrew ..." she hesitated, now caught by more recent memory. There was that one illuminating moment on the day she had prayed for healing. At the moment of discovery had come the sure understanding that now filled her thoughts. It was she who possessed all needed things—light, understanding, truth.

Because God in His gracious giving had given her himself—light. Now she was seeing Andrew groping—blind, weak, bound. That expression on his face—the features were sagging in fear and defeat. Wasn't he spiralling downward, ever deeper, while she was free and her movement was upward? It was Jesus Christ who had given her freedom. And with the freedom? The verse moved into her thoughts, ". . . and we ought to lay down our lives . . ." She sighed and now she was speaking to that Presence, saying, "I have to prove all those things, the forgiveness—my forgiving him and the healing—that I really do walk in love, don't I?"

"What?" Andrew asked, taking a tentative step. She realized the gun was drooping in her hands. She raised it and then laughed. She was knowing it was first irony and then real joy. "You're tetched," he whispered. "All those things that happened to you—"

"Ah, Andrew, 'twas no fault of yours that I wasn't. 'Twas all of God that I am whole and free and alive." The freedom rushed through her and she actually chuckled. "I'm holding this gun now so's you'll listen. See, it was like the Lord Jesus Christ threw a bucket of understanding over me the other day. For a year I'd been hating you, groveling in the ugliness. There was scarcely a day that I didn't remember those horrors and think of my dead baby without wishing I could tear the heart out of you. And then . . . Then there was a moment with God, and all that hate changed."

She looked at him and saw the curiosity in his eyes even as he licked his lips nervously. As she watched, she was accepting the sure knowledge that there was no way she could walk out of the cabin alive. There had to be a death, and hers was already completed—on the cross with her Lord Jesus. It was the only way. In the face of Jesus, the other was unthinkable.

Again the mirth rose in her and she couldn't resist saying, "These are the things I've wanted to say to you, Andrew, since years ago I first began discovering the way. But never did you quite allow me to say it all. I was bound by fear then. Now *you* are bound—by this gun, and you'll have to listen.

"At the moment I told Jesus Christ that I would forgive you and I would love you, there was this pure vision I was seeing. Andrew, you are caught in a web, being pulled down. You must stop it before it is too late. Don't you see? Every moment, every breath you take moves you farther away."

"From you?"

"No, from truth. From the possibility of reaching out and taking that beautiful thing Jesus Christ is extending toward you."

She could see that momentarily he was stunned, intrigued. "And what is it?"

"His salvation. It is *by grace* you are saved, through believing and accepting. You see, it's all a free gift. Salvation is something Jesus Christ has won for you. There's nothing He wants from you except your love and loyalty." She was whispering now, "Could the proud Andrew ever surrender his kingdom and his godhead for the privilege of being a love slave?" There was no longer any laughter in her; it was the ultimate question.

And, seeing something in it all, he whispered again, "What is it?"

"I'm fearing for you," she whispered back. "I never thought in my life I would have a moment's further emotion for you, but now I'm seeing the torture in you and I'm catching a glimpse of how much it will be. Andrew, when you see Him, what will you say?"

He knew who she meant and she saw the wondering in his eyes.

"We don't create our salvation, our righteousness," she whispered; "it's a beautiful gift. All we need do is tell Him that we want it. But you have to be willing to tear your heart out and give it to Him!"

He still hung motionless, unmoving, caught. She glanced down at the gun and took a deep breath. While it was still shivering through her, she turned and tossed the gun out the window. "You don't give with a gun in your hand," she said as she turned back and held out her empty hand.

There was his movement and the sound at the window at the same time. "Hold it, Jacobson, or I'll kill you on the spot."

Men surged into the room while Rebecca and Andrew stood motionless, staring at each other.

And then there was Joshua. His white, strained face came between them. "Rebecca, are you all right?" She must touch him, erase those lines on his face.

She was nodding her head slowly, trying to move her lips while he held her close. "I know," he whispered; "we were listening. It's life after you'd given it up. But it's life, too, for me, my darling wife."

He was still holding her close while she murmured, "It was Jesus, my Lord. He did take care of it all. Oh, Joshua, if this had happened a week ago, I'd have shot him without a second thought!"

Now the jumble of angry words in the room rose and they turned. "You lied." "False pretenses." "An innocent woman."

Joshua released her and stepped forward. Resting his rifle against the broken fireplace, he said to Andrew, "There's only one way to handle this. You're going back to town with us. We'll have you before the judge to tell your story. And then we'll find out what justice is."

For a moment, just a moment, Joshua half turned to look at Rebecca. She heard the shout, the warning, and Joshua was shoved. There was a quick movement in the fading light.

With Joshua's rifle held high, with his left arm circling Joshua's neck, Andrew backed toward the door. Norton, calm and speaking softly said, "But you said you were in the right. You claimed your special hold on heaven gave you the right to plural marriage. You're saying that we poor mortals know nothin' about the right way to live. Seems since you were so certain about it all at noon today, then you'd be *proud* to have your day in court."

They were nearly through the door when Joshua thrust himself against Andrew's extended arm, pinning it against the doorjamb. The rifle clattered to the ground and Joshua lurched across the room directly in the path of the men scrambling for the door.

Rushing against the tide of men, Rebecca threw herself down beside Joshua. Voiceless, her hands moved over his face, now pulling him close, still wordless.

"Oh, Becka, my little Becky—it's all over." He got to his feet, lifting her with him. "Let's get out of here right now. Those fellows will bring him in. You're my responsibility, my only responsibility."

As Rebecca raised her arms, they heard the gunshot. Slowly she lowered them. Joshua moved first, turning toward the door. "Someone's hurt."

There was the sharp thud of hooves and the whinny of a horse. "Must have been Jacobson shooting. He's got away." He looked down at Rebecca and she saw the fear in his eyes.

She clasped his arms, "Joshua, it's for me you're fearing. You think I can't live with knowing he's still out there. That isn't so. If the healing touch Jesus Christ poured out on me this last week wasn't enough to convince me I'll never fear that man again, then most certainly the miracle He's worked in me just this night would be enough. I could have shot that man—it would have been so easy. But I knew, sure as I knew He was right here with me, there was no longer a hate in me." Her eyes were searching his face. "Do you believe in miracles?"

He was blinking his eyes. "Becky, I'm seeing one."

Outside the door a dry branch snapped. Joshua stepped in front of Rebecca and said, "Who's there?"

Eagle stepped through the door, hesitated. They saw blood, "Eagle!" Rebecca gasped. "You've been shot. On, my dear, let me help." She flew at him, seeing the gash in his shirt, the blood flowing.

"He shot you!" Joshua caught the man and led him to the bed of blankets. Carefully he eased him down, saying, "Becky, is there something to bind around him? He's bleedin' pretty bad."

Quickly she looked around, "Oh, Andrew's bundle." She crossed the room, knelt close to the fire and tore open the pack.

Joshua leaned over Eagle and ripped open his shirt, seeing the wound as he leaned closer. "Eagle, that's no gunshot wound," he said. "A knife did that—what happened?"

"He ran into the bushes, no out." His voice was soft and he gestured with his hand, making a downward motion. "He had knife. I had gun."

"Eagle," Joshua interrupted sharply, "that's enough. Say no more." They stared into each other's eyes and then Eagle turned his head with a tired sigh.

"What happened, what is it?" Solali was clinging to the sagging door, staring at Eagle. "Is he dying?" she gasped. Without waiting for an answer she flew across the room and fell to her knees beside the bed. Her voice dropped to a crooning whisper in Paiute.

"Solali," Joshua protested, "how did you get here?" But he stopped immediately when he realized she would come after the two dearest people to her on earth. "He's only been nicked, but he's losing blood. Move back, and let's get this taken care of. Becky, have you found something?"

"Here's a clean shirt." As she crossed the room she was busy tearing it into strips. "Here's water in this bottle."

Solali elbowed Joshua out of the way and reached for the water. Joshua and Rebecca hung over the bed as Solali worked. The pain on Eagle's face eased and a faint smile crept to his lips as Solali continued to croon.

"What's she saying?" Joshua asked Rebecca.

"I don't know, but it sounds about like the crooning she was doing for Matthew's baby, trying to get him to sleep." Joshua chuckled. He turned to the doorway.

Rebecca had heard it, too. The subdued murmur of voices and the crunch of feet on stones. The rest of the men filed into the room.

Their serious faces centered on Eagle. "We'd a'been more on our toes if we'd a'known the Mormon'd be so violent."

Joshua said, "Got away, huh?"

They exchanged sheepish glances. "Fine trackers we are. If Norton here's going to be runnin' for sheriff, we're going to have to take him out and teach him a few things." They shifted uneasily.

"Sure sorry your Indian friend got it. Is it serious? We could fix a sling."

"Naw," Joshua said. "It's not much more'n a good nick. Shouldn't have been standin' in the way."

They exchanged looks. "Well, it weren't our bunch; nary a shot fired here. Never did get close enough. We stuck around the horses, waiting for action there."

"But what has happened to him?" Rebecca asked, looking around the circle.

"I've a feeling he's a hightailing it over the mountains and won't stop until he gets clear to Utah Territory. He sure ain't around here. We did a good job of beatin' the bushes."

Rebecca looked from one man to the other. Norton touched his hat and said, "Ma'am, I'm right sorry. I know it isn't a good feeling to know he's still a'runnin' free, but—"

"No, please. I'm just thanking you for helping. I'm not fearin', and someday I'll be able to talk about it."

Chambers spoke up. "If you're wantin', we can get a posse together tomorrow when it's light."

"Through this brush. The trail would be dead by morning," Joshua said shortly.

"Right you are." The men looked relieved. "Well, if there's no more we can do here, we'd better be gettin' on home. There's milkin' yet to be done. It's a fair piece down the hill."

Rebecca was smiling and blinking at the tears. Milking. "How can I ever thank you enough?" She looked around at the men. They were embarrassed, curious, she could see, but open.

"Aw, ma'am, I reckon if you'd bake us a big cake and put on a pot of coffee one of these cool evenings and invite us over, we'd all consider it even."

The men filed out the door. Joshua turned to Rebecca. "What did you say?"

"I said 'milking.' They're going to home to milk." Her voice caught. "Oh, Joshua, this afternoon when we left the church, I was riding on a high tide of fear and certain death. I was sure I'd never see you again, even while I tried to hope. Now it's back to life as usual. What a strange and wonderful blessing life is! Milking." She took a deep shaky breath.

"While I was hanging on that horse, thinking it was the end of everything important, I kept thinking about the chances I'd missed."

"What do you mean?" he asked in a low voice.

"The times I could have told you how much I love you, how much I've appreciated you down through all these years. And then the way you rescued me—" She stopped, tears choking her, and then she continued, "—rescued me from all that. The thought of not being able to say it because I had delayed— well—" There was another shaky breath and then with a smile she continued, "I'll make it up. You'll see a wife who doesn't hardly let you out of her sight."

For a moment longer Joshua stood looking down at her and she watched the tight lines on his face soften and disappear as a slow smile crept across it. "And I want to hear it all. Maybe we'd better get started."

He turned and walked to the bed. "Solali, can you help get Eagle back down this mountain to the house? Seems the best way is to ride on his horse with him. I don't reckon he's too bad off, but I'd hate for him to faint from loss of blood and pitch off his mount." Rebecca followed Joshua to the bedside. She could see that Eagle's eyes were sparkling in the firelight.

The impulse was impossible to resist. She addressed Solali. "Maybe you'd better be using the time to tell him about how you decided you really want to go home and live among your people." She paused to shake her head ruefully, "Why you'd prefer that to being a white man's wife, I'll never know, but—"

"Rebecca!" Solali gasped.

"What?" Rebecca asked innocently. "He can't understand

English, so it's all right. And you can take all the time you want to tell him that you really love him."

"Rebecca," Joshua chided, his voice full of laughter. Rebecca darted a quick look at Eagle. He was grinning up at Solali as he held out his hands to be helped to his feet. When he was up and moving slowly toward the door, Joshua turned. "I'm thinkin' he doesn't need to lean that hard," he drawled.

Now Joshua slipped his arm across Rebecca's shoulder and pulled her close. "Did kissin' fit in with all those regrets?" She laughed up at him as she stood on tiptoe for his kiss.

The last embers of the fire were winking out and Joshua said, "Becky, my dear wife, let's go home."

Outside the moon was riding high in the sky, ready to accompany them down the mountain. "Looks like Solali and Eagle aren't the only ones who'll have to ride double," Joshua said. "There's only one horse left. They've taken the other ones with them."

Rebecca lingered. Moonlight was gilding the fir trees and turning to silver the decaying boards of the old shack. Joshua followed her glance and said, "The old place won't stand more'n another couple of winter snows."

"I'm glad. I don't want to be reminded of the way I felt when I walked into that place." She turned and looked up at him in the moonlight. "It was such a lonesome feeling. I could see the suppertime smoke rising above the trees. The setting sun made me think of all the cozy settling down that needs to be done at night. All those people were snug in their homes with family and I was alone on the mountainside."

"Were you really?"

"No," she whispered. "I know you want me to say I realized my God was here, and I did. But I guess what I'm saying is that until then, I didn't understand how much I really wanted us to be a family. Joshua and Rebecca."

"Then let's get going, Mrs. Smyth. I have a lot of work to do yet tonight."

She stopped in the path. "Work!" she cried in dismay. "Work? Whatever do you have to do tonight?"

"That pretty wedding dress has some drawbacks. I've been